CONTEMPORARY CHINA'S SOCIETY

By Li Wen

 China Intercontinental Press

图书在版编目（C I P）数据
当代中国社会：英文 / 李文著；王丽，李莉译. -- 北京：五洲传播出版社，2014.6
（当代中国系列 / 武力主编）
ISBN 978-7-5085-2794-9

Ⅰ.①当… Ⅱ.①李… ②王… ③李… Ⅲ.①社会发展–概况–中国–英文 Ⅳ.①D668

中国版本图书馆 CIP 数据核字 (2014) 第 124443 号

当代中国系列丛书

主　　编：武　力
出 版 人：荆孝敏
统　　筹：付　平

当代中国社会

著　　者：李　文
译　　者：王　丽　李　莉
责任编辑：王　峰
图片提供：中新社　CFP　东方 IC　FOTOE
装帧设计：丰饶文化传播有限责任公司
出版发行：五洲传播出版社
地　　址：北京市海淀区北三环中路 31 号生产力大楼 B 座 7 层
邮　　编：100088
电　　话：010-82005927，82007837
网　　址：www.cicc.org.cn
承 印 者：中煤涿州制图印刷厂北京分厂
版　　次：2014 年 6 月第 1 版第 1 次印刷
开　　本：787×1092 毫米 1/16
印　　张：17.25
字　　数：200 千字
定　　价：118.00 元

Contents

Foreword

In the 20th century, two historic events in China have affected the entire world. One is the founding of the People's Republic of China under a socialist system, which fundamentally changed the political landscape in East Asia and the world. The other is China's reform and opening up, upon which a socialist market economy has been built, enabling its economy to enjoy sustained rapid development and fundamentally rebuilding the economy of East Asia and the globe. Both events are of historical significance in achieving the great "Chinese Dream"- realization of national rejuvenation, national prosperity and people's well-being.

In the 21st century China has maintained its development momentum from the previous two decades. It has actively dealt with profound changes in the international situation while maintaining fast development at home and overcoming all sorts of risks, hardship and challenges to achieve an historic economic leap. It has made a series of new historic achievements to offer a solid basis for building a moderately prosperous society in an all-round way. China's GDP has rocketed from the world's sixth-largest to the second-largest.. Social productivity, economic strength and scientific and technological strength

Tian'anmen Square in Beijing on the evening of the National Day.

have made a big step forward. In the meantime, living standards, income levels and social security have undergone unprecedented progress. What's more, comprehensive national strength, international competitiveness and international influence have increased dramatically. China is displaying a new historic look. As is widely recognized, this is a time during which China's economy, democracy, culture and social stability are experiencing constant development. It is a time when people's livelihoods are guaranteed and improved through great efforts with more tangible benefits available. At the same time, China's economic structure is facing deep-rooted problems, such as economic development severely restricted by resources and environment, unbalanced economic and social development, an expanding gap between the rich and the poor, intense and frequent explosions of interest disputes and social contradictions. Due to the slow recovery of the global economy and increasing pressure on the domestic economy, more contradictions and problems have become increasingly pronounced during China's development.

This book mainly covers the development of Chinese society since the advent of the 21st century and references the second half of the 20th century when necessary. Except when specifically noted, the data quoted are sourced from websites of the National Bureau of Statistics and relevant ministries and commissions of China.

俺环保，
俺快乐！
More fun,
without

From a Moderately Prosperous Society to China Dream

The term "society" may refer to both "greater society", i.e. the all-inclusive "human society" which covers economics, politics, culture etc., or the "aggregate" or "community" evolved from humanity's interactions, and the "small society", i.e. the "social community" opposite to government, or the territory parallel to economics, politics and culture. This book introduces Chinese society from the perspective of "small society" and covers the social structure, construction and management as well as the living conditions and thinking in society. The moderately prosperous society proposed by Deng Xiaoping, chief architect of China's reform and opening-up, refers to "greater society". Now let's examine the general situation of "small society" in China from the aspect of "greater society".

From Substeces to a Moderately Prosperous Society

The "Moderately Prosperous Society" and "Three-Step Development Strategy"

Half a century ago, the first generation of leaders of New China proposed a two-step economic development plan. First they called for the establishment of an independent, comparatively complete industrial system and national economic system. Second, they aimed to achieve modernizations in agriculture,

December 18–22, 1978, the Third Plenary Session of the Eleventh Central Committee of the CPC was held in Beijing. This is a turning point in the Party's history since the founding of New China. Deng Xiaoping made a speech at the meeting, called on the people to emancipate the mind, to seek truth from facts, and to look ahead in unity.

industry, national defense and science and technology, in order to enable the Chinese economy to take the lead in the world. When reforms in China began at the end of 1970s, the first goal was generally achieved, but there was still far to go to achieve the second goal. The moderately prosperous society is a new concept for the second goal proposed by Deng, who used an old saying with a new connotation. During his meetings with the Japanese prime ministers in December 1979 Deng pointed out, "The four modernizations we are striving to achieve are modernizations with Chinese characteristics. Our concept of the four modernizations is different from yours. By achieving the four modernizations, we mean achieving a comparative prosperity." Meeting with Japan's prime minister in March 1984, Deng said: "If, by the end of the century, the annual gross value of industrial and agricultural output is quadrupled, and the average per capita GNP reaches US$ 800, then we shall have a society in which people lead a fairly comfortable life. Realizing this society is what we call Chinese-style modernization."

Different from the previous "four modernizations", the "moderately prosperous society", neither affluent nor poor, is a pragmatic goal for gradual development. According to statistics of the World Bank, in 1978, China was still a low-income country. Per capita GDP was merely US$ 155, about 7.9% of the global average, ranking 133rd out of 135 countries and regions worldwide. Per capita GNI was merely US$ 190, about 10.2% of the global average, ranking 175th out of 188 countries and regions worldwide. The Engel coefficient1 stood at a high 67.7% in rural areas and 57.5% in urban areas. And one quarter of the Chinese population (about 250 million people) were extremely poverty-stricken people with inadequate food and clothing.

Therefore, Deng Xiaoping proposed his three-step development strategy. "Our goal for the first step is to reach, by 1990, a per capita GNP of US$ 500, that is, double the 1980 figure of $250. The goal for the second step is, by the turn of the century, to reach a per capita GNP of $1,000. When we reach that goal, China will have shaken off poverty and achieved relative prosperity. When the total GNP exceeds \$1 trillion, the national strength will have increased considerably, although per capita GNP would still be very low. The goal we have set for the third step is the most important one: quadrupling the \$1 trillion figure of the year 2000 within another 30 to 50 years. That will mean a per capita GNP of roughly \$4,000 -- in other words, a medium standard of living."

In 1997, China quadrupled its per capita GDP ahead of schedule. By 2000, the Chinese government announced that the people had started to live moderately prosperous lives. In 2007, at the 17th CPC Congress, the Party set forth the new requirement of quadrupling per capita GDP of the year 2000 by 2020 in addition to quadrupling the GDP for the same period proposed in the 16th CPC Congress, which means that China's achievement of "a medium standard of living" would come much earlier than Deng had predicted.

The 17th National Congress of Communist Party of China was convened in Beijing from Oct. 15th, 2007 to Oct. 21st, 2007.

Levels and Standards of a Moderately Prosperous Society

In detail, what would the moderately prosperous society that China would achieve by the end of 20th century look like? According to Deng's prognostication in 1984, it would be like the situation in the economically developed region south of Yangtze River Delta at that time: "First, people will not swarm to Shanghai and Beijing, just like the southern Jiangsu locals who take delight in local life. Second, per capita residential area will reach about 20 square meters. Third, primary and secondary school education will be popularized through government investment. Fourth, the food supply, consumption supply and consumer electronics supply will meet people's demands. Fifth, people's spiritual levels will be greatly improved, and illegal conduct and criminal acts will drastically decrease." Thus, achieving a moderately prosperous society is not to simply quadruple the per capita GDP. Six years later, the 7th plenary session of the 13th

China has been fast moving from a traditional agricultural country to a modern urban country.

Table 1-1-1
National Standards for a Moderately Prosperous Society

Index type	Index name	Index critical value			
		Unit	1980	Standard for moderately prosperous ociety	Weight
I. Economic Level					
	1.Per capita GDP	yuan	778	2500	14
II. Material Life					48
Income	2.Per capita income				16
	(1) Urban per capita disposable income	yuan	974	2400	6
	(2) Rural per capital net income	yuan	315	1200	10
Residence	3. Per capita residential level				12
	(1) Urban per capita usage area	sq.m.	5.5	12	5
	(2) Urban per capita residential area for steel, brick and wooden buildings	sq.m.	4.5	15	7
Nutrition	4.Per capita protein ADI	Grams	50	75	6
Transport	5.Urban transport status				8

	(1) Area of paved road per 10,000 urban residents		2.8	8	3
	(2) Proportion of rural villages with highway access	%	50	85	5
Structure	6. Engel coefficient	%	60	50	6
III. Population Quality					14
Culture	7.Adult literacy rate	%	68	85	6
Health	8.Per capita life expectancy	yuan	68	70	4
	9.Infant mortality rate	‰	34.7	31	4
IV. Spiritual Life					10
	10.Percentage of education and recreation expenses	%	3	11	5
	11.TV popularity percentage	%	11.9	100	5
V. Living Environment					14
	12.Forest coverage	%	12	15	7
	13.Percentages of counties meeting primary health standards in rural areas	%		100	7
Total	16 indices				100

China began to promote the new socialist countryside construction in 2006. The picture shows a mountain village in Ganxian County, Jiangxi Province.

CPC Congress adopted "The Suggestion of CCCPC on Developing National Economic and Social Development Ten-year Plan and the Eighth Five-year Plan" and added further definition: "a moderately prosperous society refers to people's life quality further improving based upon adequate supply of food and clothing, and people are well-fed and well-clothed. It includes the improvement of material life, spiritual life, social welfare and labor environment." By the end of the 20th century, "the people lived in a moderately prosperous society with more living materials, a more reasonable consumption structure, noticeably improved residential conditions, a richer cultural life, a continuously improving health level and social facilities."

In order to measure the level of a moderately prosperous society, the former National Planning Commission, the National Statistics Bureau and other ministries developed different evaluation standards for the whole country, urban areas and rural areas (See Tables 1-1-1, 1-1-2 and 1-1-3 respectively). The national basic standard consists of 16 indices, while urban and rural standards make adjustment based on these indices to cater for the objectively large gaps

Table 1-1-2 Urban Standards for a Moderately Prosperous Society				
Index	**Unit**	**Index Critical Value**		**Weight**
		In 1980	**Value for Moderately Prosperous Society**	
I. Economic level				21
1. Per capita GDP	yuan	1750	5000	12
2. Percentage of tertiary industry	%	20.6	40	9
II. Material life				37
3. Per capita disposable income	yuan	974	2400	15
4. Per capita housing area	sq.m.	5.5	12	10
5. Per capita protein ADI	gram	60	75	5
6. Enge'l coefficient	%	62	50	7
III. Population Quality				12
7. Average life expectancy	year	67	70	5
8. High school enrollment rate	%	70	90	7
IV. Spiritual Life				12
9. TV popularity percentage	%	58	100	5
10. Percentage of culture, education and recreation expenses	%	6	16	7
V. Living environment and social security				18
11. Per capita green space	sq.m.	3	9	9
12. The number of registered criminal cases per 10,000 people	case		20	9
Total				100

Table 1-1-3 The National Rural Residents for a Moderately Prosperous Society				
Index	**Unit**	**Weight**	**Food and Clothing Supply Value**	**Prosperity Value**
I. Income distribution		35		
1. Per capita net income	yuan	30	300	1200
2. Gini coefficient	%	5	0.2	0.3-0.4
II. Material life		25		
3. Engel's coefficient	%	6	60	≤50
4. Protein ADI	gram	9	47	75
5. Clothing consumption expenses	yuan	3	27	70
6. Percentage of steel or wood structured housing	%	7	43	80
III. Spiritual life		12		
7. TV popularity percentage	set/100 households	6	1	70
8. Percentage of culture and service expenses	%	6	2	10
IV. Population quality		9		
9. Per capita life expectancy	year	4	68	70
10. Average education level of labor force	year	5	6	8
V. Living environment		11		
11. Percentage of administrative villages with highway access	%	3	50	85
12. Rate of clean water access	%	3	50	90
13. Percentage of households with electricity	%	3	50	95

14. Percentage of administrative villages with telephone services	%	2	50	70
VI. Social insurance and social security		8		
15. Percentage of population enjoying the "five guarantees"	%	4	50	90
16. The number of registered criminal cases per 10,000 people	cases	4	5	≤20
Total		100		

between both. Most of the indices in the tables, except those which reflect economic development level, are directly related to social construction and life. Based upon calculations, the national realization level of a moderately prosperous society reached 48% in 1996 and 96% in 2000. By 2000, three indices had failed to meet their respective standards Rural per capita net income was 1,066 yuan, 85% of the index, per capital protein ADI was 75 grams, 90% of the index, and 80% of relevant counties met the rural primary health standard. The eastern China generally met the standards for a moderately prosperous society, central China met 78% of the standards and the western China met 56%. For the same period from 1991 to 2000, the Engel coefficient decreased from 53.8% to 39.4% in urban areas and from 57.6% to 49.1% in rural areas. China's achievements in poverty relief and development are also eye-catching, its poverty-stricken population dropped by 220 million in rural areas2. Over the past two decades, China is the country that made the greatest contributions to global poverty-relief efforts, and China's innovative large-scale poverty-relief activities offer constructive cases for global poverty-relief actions, according to the World Bank.

Comprehensive Prosperity

The New Three-step Strategy

It was obvious that China's "general prosperity" at the end of the 20th century was just a low-level, material consumption-focused prosperity with unbalanced development. By the end of 2000, China's per capita GDP was only $800, falling into the category of middle- and low-income countries. In total, 30 million people were still suffereing from the problems of inadequate food and clothing across China, and some urban people were living below the minimum subsistence level. Quite a few areas in western China had a long way to go to reach general prosperity, which was a hard nut to crack. Then, the conflict between people's increasing material and cultural demands and backward social production was still the major contradiction. China was still backward in productivity, science and technology and education and had a long way to go in industrialization and modernization. The urban-rural dual economic structure had not changed, and the expanding gap between regions was not reversing. China still had many poor people, a growing population, an aging population, higher pressure in employment and social security and increasingly sharper contradictions between socioeconomic development and the environment and natural resources. China still faced pressures from developed countries who had economic, scientific and technological advantages. The economic system and other administrative systems were defective and some problems in the development of democracy, a legal system, morality and ideology could not be neglected. Long-term efforts were still required to consolidate and improve the prosperity achieved by that time.

There are still large gaps between the level of economic development of the central and western regions in China and that of the east developed regions.

Therefore, in 1997 the 15th National Congress of the CPC elaborated upon the third step of Deng's three-step strategy, and promoted the new three-step strategy. The goal for the first half of the 21st century was: within the first decade, the gross national product must be double that of the 2000, allowing people to enjoy an even more comfortable life. A more or less ideal socialist market economy will have come into being. With the efforts to be made in another decade when the Party celebrates its centenary, the national economy will be more developed and the various systems will be further improved. By the middle of the 21st century, when New China celebrates its centenary, the modernization program will have been accomplished by and large and China will have become a prosperous, strong, democratic and culturally advanced socialist country. So, a development plan of comprehensive prosperity at a higher level is coming into shape based upon low-level general prosperity.

Comprehensive Prosperity and the Current Achievements

In the year 2000, the 5th plenary session of the 15th National Congress of the CPC announced that "China will enter the new development stage of comprehensively building a moderately prosperous society and accelerating socialist modernization to realize a new milestone in the historical development of the Chinese nation." In 2002, based upon the new three-step strategy proposed at the 15th National Congress of the CPC, the 16th National Congress of the CPC defined the objectives as "building a well-off society of a higher standard in an all-round way in this period to the benefit of well over one billion people. We will further develop the economy, improve democracy, advance science and education, enrich culture, foster social harmony and upgrade the quality of life for people" in the first two decades of the 21st century. The objectives for the economy and livelihood were made clear: "On the basis of optimized structure and better economic returns, efforts will be made to quadruple the GDP of the year 2000 by 2020, and China's overall national strength and international competitiveness will increase markedly. We will achieve industrialization and establish a full-fledged socialist market economy and a more open and viable economic system. The proportion of the urban population will go up considerably and the trend of widening differences between industry and agriculture, between urban and rural areas and between regions will be reversed step by step. We will have a fairly sound social security system. There will be a higher rate of employment. People will have more family property and live a more prosperous life." The 16th Party Congress also put forward the moderately prosperous society's objectives for politics, culture, environment and other areas. In 2007, the 17th Party Congress set forth the new requirement of quadrupling per capita GDP of the year 2000 by 2020 in addition to quadrupling GDP for the same period proposed in the 16th Party Congress. The evolution of objectives for a moderately prosperous society proposed at the 16th Party Congress and enriched at the 17th and 18th Party Congresses indicated that targets were being set higher and higher to realize the development from a middle or low economy toward a middle and upper

Table 1-2-1 GDP Comparison Between Chinese Mainland and Major Global Economies

Unit: GDP /$ 100mil., Percentage of World Total/ %

Rank	2000			1990			1980		
	Countries	GDP	Percentage	Countries	GDP	Percentage	Countries	GDP	Percentage
	World	323,313	100	World	221,959	100	World	107,113	100
1	U.S.	99,515	30.78	U.S.	58,005	26.13	U.S.	27,882	26.03
2	Japan	47,312	14.63	Japan	31,037	13.98	Japan	10,870	10.15
3	Germany	18,919	5.85	Germany	15,470	6.97	Germany	8,261	7.71
4	U.K.	14,787	4.57	France	12,474	5.62	France	6,913	6.45
5	France	13,302	4.11	Italy	11,402	5.14	U.K.	5,425	5.06
6	China	11,985	3.71	U.K.	10,246	4.62	Italy	4,700	4.39
7	Italy	11,073	3.42	Canada	5,947	2.68	Canada	2,744	2.56
8	Canada	7,397	2.29	Spain	5,204	2.34	Mexico	2,266	2.12
9	Mexico	6,719	2.08	Brazil	4,650	2.09	Spain	2,244	2.09
10	Brazil	6,443	1.99	China	3,903	1.76	Argentina	2,090	1.95
11	Spain	5,820	1.80	Australia	3,238	1.46	China	2,025	1.89
12	ROK	5,334	1.65	India	3,235	1.46	India	1,814	1.69
13	India	4,764	1.47	Netherlands	2,956	1.33	Netherlands	1,772	1.65
14	Australia	3,996	1.24	Mexico	2,878	1.30	Saudi Arabia	1,640	1.53
15	Netherlands	3,862	1.19	ROK	2,704	1.22	Australia	1,629	1.52

Data source: The data were sorted based upon the *World Economy Outlook* issued in April 2013 by the IMF. Data prior to 1991 do not include the Soviet Union. If the Soviet Union is included, China's rank would be one position lower.

economy. They were also being made broader and broader, not only addressing economics, politics, culture, society and the environment, but also avoiding the slow development of rural areas hindering urban areas, of western China hindering eastern and central China. The National Bureau of Statistics created 23 indexes in six areas for a moderately prosperous society3. According to the results uncovered, the national degree of realization of comprehensive prosperity reached 80.1% in 2010, 20.5 percentage points higher than that of 2000, with an annual growth of 2.05 percentage points (see Table 1-2-2).

In the first decade of construction of comprehensive prosperity in the new century, achievements in economic development are the most eye-catching. From 2000 to 2010, China's GDP increased to 40.2 trillion yuan from 9.9 trillion yuan with an annual growth of 10.3% after deducting price factors as illustrated in Figure 1-2-1. It was not easy for China to make such an achievement during such a difficult decade of international and domestic challenges. Globally, the international financial crisis triggered by the American subprime mortgage crisis swept the world. Domestically, SARS, freezing rain and snow, the Wenchuan earthquake and other calamities and challenges were relentless. During this period, China's economic growth made an obvious contribution to global economic development. According to data from National Bureau of Statistics, from 2003 to 2011, the average annual economy growth of China was 10.7%, and that of the world was 3.9%. The proportion of China's economic aggregate to the world's total improved from 4.4% in 2002 to about 10% in 2011. And the rank of China's economic aggregate climbed from sixth in 2002 to second in 2010. According to the report by the World Bank, China's per capita GDP reached $4,260 in 2010, even less than 47% of the world average, but higher than the World Bank's benchmark of $3,976 for UMC (upper middle income) of the year, and China became a UMC economy. From 2006 to 2010, China's per capita GDP experienced growth of over 100%, which is an astonishing feat.

However, for the same period, in comparison with the economic development, China's social development was not quite satisfactory, and some

Table 1-2-2

China's Comprehensive Construction of a Moderately Prosperous Society and Achievements in Six Aspects Between 2000 and 2010

Unit %

	2000	2001	2002	2003	2004	2005	2006	2007	2008	2009	2010
Comprehensive construction of moderately prosperous society	59.6	60.7	61.8	63.0	64.8	67.2	69.9	72.8	74.7	77.5	80.1
Economic development	50.3	52.2	54.4	56.3	58.2	60.6	63.4	66.6	69.1	73.1	76.1
Social harmony	57.5	59.6	57.1	56.3	59.9	62.8	67.6	72.1	76.0	77.7	82.5
Life quality	58.3	60.7	62.9	65.5	67.7	71.5	75.0	78.4	80.0	83.7	86.4
Democracy and legal system	84.8	82.6	82.5	82.4	83.7	85.6	88.4	89.9	91.1	93.1	93.6
Culture and education	58.3	59.1	60.9	61.8	62.2	63.0	64.1	65.3	64.6	66.1	68.0
Resources and environment	65.4	64.6	66.3	67.2	67.7	69.5	70.6	72.6	75.2	76.8	78.2

Data source: *Statistical Monitoring Report on the Course of Building a Well-off Society in an All-around Way in 2007 (2011)*, Scientific Research Institute of National Bureau of Statistics

The supplies of Chinese people have become rich, and their concepts of life has also been changed due to the market economy.

indices even went down. The urban-rural gap went back from 99.8% in 2000 to 70.3% in 2010, and the Gini coefficient and social security index in 2010 were even worse than those in 2000. Eastern, central, western and northeastern China saw progress in construction of a prosperous society, but the gaps among them were still wide. Internationally speaking, China is still a developing country with per capita GDP and consumption lower than the global averages. According to UN standards, China still has 150 million poor people. Moreover, China is still unreasonable in economic structure, insufficient in public education and health care spending, incomplete in its social security system, underdeveloped in overall scientific and technological levels, low in per capita resource and energy, short in resource and energy supplies, yet high in gross consumption with severe environmental pollution. What's more, the above weighted data cannot objectively reflect the true holistic view since they focus more on the average while neglecting the great internal gaps. It is a core characteristic of constructing a moderately prosperous society to solve the problems of regional gaps, urban-rural gaps and the rich-poor gap. To solve urban-rural imbalance is pivotal to achieving industrialization, informatization, urbanization and agricultural modernization. In other words, both the crucial and most difficult part of building a moderately prosperous society is small society. It is a test that China must pass to ensure smooth continued development and avoid the "middle-income trap4".

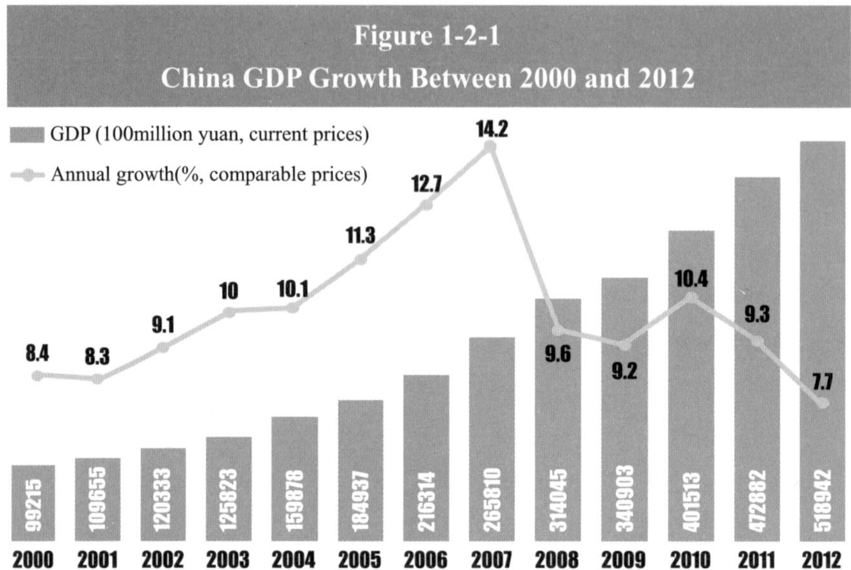

Data source: *China Statistical Yearbook* (2012) by the National Bureau of Statistics. The data in 2011 and 2012 are the data after preliminary verification.

Data source: *China Statistical Yearbook* (2012) by the National Bureau of Statistics. The data in 2011 and 2012 are the data after preliminary verification. The growth rate for 2012 is estimated by the author.

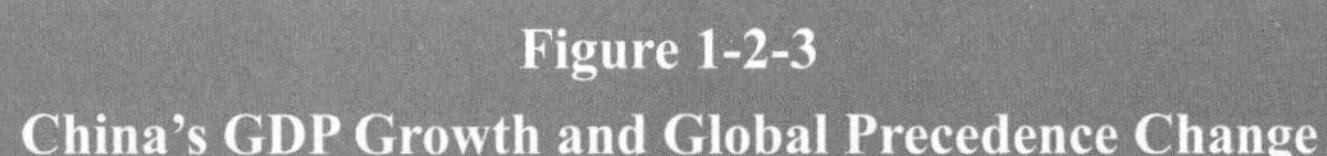

Figure 1-2-3
China's GDP Growth and Global Precedence Change

China's GDP Ranking, 2000–2011

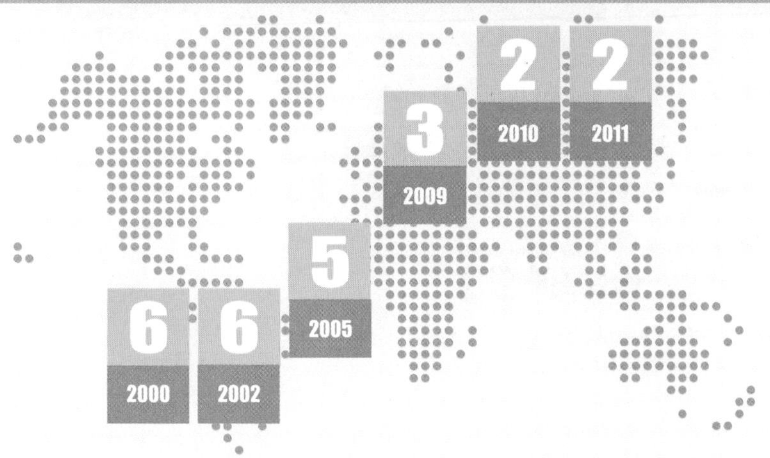

China's GDP, 2002–2011

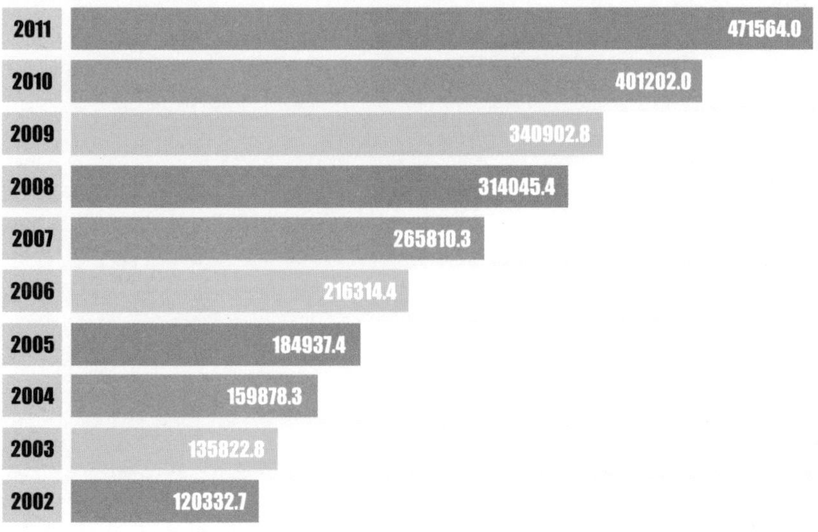

Per Capita GDP of Selected Countries in 2011

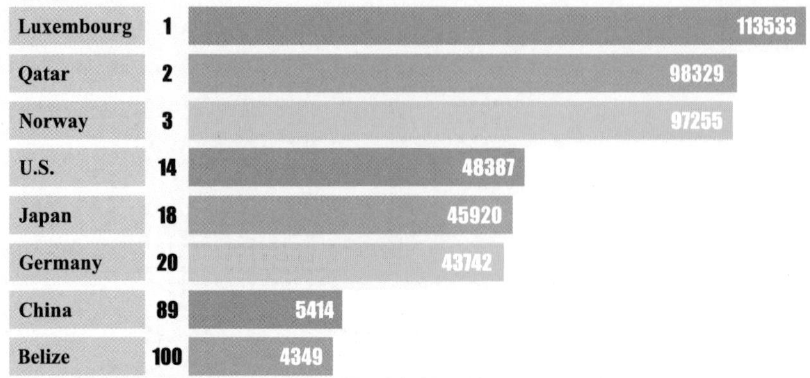

Data source: National Bureau of Statistics, UN Database, IMF's website

Quote from people.com.cn, June 4, 2012

The China Dream

Two 100-year Goals

Moderate prosperity or an all-round well-off society are both interim goals of Chinese-style modernization and indicate that modernization is a relentless pursuit of the Chinese people. It is an important mission bestowed by history to the Communist Party of China to lead the Chinese people to realize these goals.

After the founding of the New China, the first generation leadership of the CPC, with Mao Zedong as the core, had a strong desire and firm belief that China could realize industrialization and modernization, toward which persistent pursuit and exploration were conducted. They had succeeded in setting up a relatively

Deng Xiaoping wrote an inscription for the 5th anniversary of the implementation of "863" Project in 1991: "Develop high technology and realize industrialization".

complete national economic system and a wide-ranging industrial system and designed the strategic goals of realizing agricultural, industrial, national defense and technological modernizations by the end of the 20th century in the 1950s and 1960s. The twists and turns they experienced were related to their anxiousness for success and deviation from the objective rules.

Based on valuable experiences and lessons, the second generation of leadership of the CPC, with Deng Xiaoping as the core, realized that China could only achieve Chinese-style modernization by the end of the 20th century, or the relatively low-level "moderately prosperous society" and rank among the moderately developed countries by the mid-21st century. When meeting Italian guests in August 1978, Deng Xiaoping pointed out, "China is developing its economy in three steps. Two steps will be taken in this century, to reach the point where our people have adequate food and clothing and lead a fairly comfortable life. The third step, which will take us 30 to 50 years into the next century, is to reach the level of the moderately developed countries. These are our strategic objectives and our high ambitions." This goal become the common understanding of the Party and was written into the report of the 13th National Congress of the CPC. Since then the goal was iterated from the 14th National Congress to the 18th National Congress of the CPC. New goals were put forward on the basis of completing or largely completing the goals of the previous stage. What has not changed are the general plan and the ultimate pursuit of basically realizing the goal of building a moderately prosperous society when the Party marks the 100th anniversary of the founding of the CPC and the goal of modernization when China celebrates its 100th anniversary of the founding of New China. The general plan and ultimate pursuit can be summarized by the statement of the new generation of leadership of the CPC, with Xi Jinping as secretary general, as the "Chinese Dream", that is, to have economic prosperity, national renewal and people being well-off (See Table 1-3-1).

Table 1-3-1
From the Moderately Prosperous Society to the Chinese Dream

Time	Content	Source
1987	China is developing its economy in three steps. Two steps will be taken in this century, to reach the point where our people have adequate food and clothing and lead a fairly comfortable life. The third step, which will take us 30 to 50 years into the next century, is to reach the level of the moderately developed countries. These are our strategic objectives and our high ambitions.	*Selected Works of Deng Xiao Ping*, Volume III, P251
The 13th National Congress of the CPC	After the Third Plenary Session of the 11th National Congress of the CPC, the strategic plan of economic development is basically divided into three steps. The first step is to double the GNP of that of the year of 1980 to solve the problems of food and clothing. The task has been largely realized. The second step is to grow the GNP by two times by the end of this century to allow our people to lead a fairly comfortable life. The third step is to reach the point where GPD reaches the level of the moderately developed countries by the mid-21st century, with our people living a well-off life and modernization largely realized. Then we will march forward on this basis.	Report at the 13th National Congress of the CPC
The 14th National Congress of the CPC	The period between now and the middle of the next century will be a most important and precious time for making our country prosperous and for advancing socialism. We have difficult tasks to accomplish, and we bear grave responsibilities. In the 1990s we must establish a preliminary new economic structure and attain the objective of the second stage of development: a relatively comfortable level of life for all our people. In another 20 years, when we mark the 100th anniversary of the founding of the Party, a whole set of more mature and complete management systems will have taken shape in every field of work. Thus, in the middle of the next century, when we celebrate the 100th anniversary of the founding of the People's Republic of China, we shall have attained the objective of the third stage: the basic realization of socialist modernization.	Report at the 14th National Congress of the CPC

The 15th National Congress of the CPC	Looking into the next century, we have set our goals as follows: In the first decade, the gross national product will double that of the year 2000, the people will enjoy an even more comfortable life and a more or less ideal socialist market economy will have come into being. With the efforts to be made in another decade when the Party celebrates its centenary, the national economy will be more developed and the various systems will be further improved. By the middle of the next century when the People's Republic celebrates its centenary, the modernization program will have been accomplished by and large and China will have become a prosperous, strong, democratic and culturally advanced socialist country.	Report at the 15th National Congress of the CPC
The Fifth Plenary Session of the 15th National Congress of the CPC	Beginning from the dawn of the new century, China will enter into a new stage of building a moderately prosperous society in an all-round way and accelerating the socialist modernization.... We have realized the strategic objectives of the first two steps of modernization. The economy and society have enjoyed all-round development and the people's livelihood has reached the level of moderate prosperity. The third step is launched. This is a new milestone in the history of the Chinese people.	Suggestions of the Central Committee of the CPC on Making up the 10th Five-Year Plan for the National Economic and Social Development
The 16th National Congress of the CPC	The objectives of building a well-off society in an all-round way are as follows: -- On the basis of optimized structure and better economic returns, efforts will be made to quadruple the GDP of the year 2000 by 2020, and China's overall national strength and international competitiveness will increase markedly. We will achieve industrialization and establish a full-fledged socialist market economy and a more open and viable economic system. The proportion of urban population will go up considerably and the trend of widening differences between industry and agriculture, between urban and rural areas and between regions will be reversed step by step. We will have a fairly sound social security system. There will be a higher rate of employment. People will have more family property and lead more prosperous lives	Report at the 16th National Congress of the CPC
The 17th National Congress of the CPC	We must meet new and higher requirements for China's development on the basis of the goal of building a moderately prosperous society in all respects set at the Sixteenth Congress. - Promote balanced development to ensure sound and rapid economic growth. The development pattern will be significantly transformed. We will quadruple the per capita GDP of the year 2000 by 2020 through optimizing the economic structure and improving economic returns while reducing consumption of resources and protecting the environment.	Report at the 17th National Congress of the CPC

The 18th National Congress of the CPC	We must work hard to meet the following new requirements while working to fulfill the goal of building a moderately prosperous society in all respects set forth at the Sixteenth and Seventeenth National Congresses of the Party. – The economy should maintain sustained and sound development. Major progress should be made in changing the growth model. On the basis of making China's development much more balanced, coordinated and sustainable, we should double its 2010 GDP and per capita income for both urban and rural residents.......	Report at the 18th National Congress of the CPC
Since the 18th National Congress of the CPC	Now we are discussing the Chinese Dream. I think that achieving the great rejuvenation of the Chinese nation is the greatest Chinese dream in modern times. Because the dream carries a long-cherished wish of generations of Chinese people. It reflects the interests of the Chinese people as a whole, and it's a common expectation of the Chinese nation.	Remarks of Xi Jinping on visiting the exhibition of Road to Revival on November 29, 2012
	The great goal of building a moderately prosperous society in all respects, building a prosperous, democratic, civilized and harmonious socialist modern nation, and realizing the Chinese dream of achieving great rejuvenation of the Chinese nation is to achieve the national prosperity and revitalization and bring about the happiness of the people. This not only reflects the ideal of the Chinese people, but also shows the glorious tradition of our forefathers' persistent pursuit to progresses.	Remarks of Xi Jinping at the First Meeting of the 12th National People's Congress on March 17, 2013
	Achieving the great rejuvenation of the Chinese nation is a long-cherished wish of generations of Chinese people.	Xi Jinping receives interview of BRICS media on March 19, 2013
	The main goals we set for China are as follows: By 2020, China's GDP and per capita incomes for urban and rural residents will double the 2010 figures, and the building of a moderately prosperous society in all respects will be completed. By the mid-21st century, China will be turned into a modern socialist country that is prosperous, strong, democratic, culturally advanced and harmonious; and the Chinese dream, namely, the great renewal of the Chinese nation, will be realized. Looking ahead, we are full of confidence in China's future.	Keynote speech of Xi Jinping at the opening plenary of Boao Forum 2013 on April 7, 2013

Since the 18th National Congress of the CPC	We have set the future goals that are to build a moderately prosperous society when we mark the 100th anniversary of the founding of the Party and grow China into a prosperous, strong, democratic and culturally advanced socialist country when the People's Republic celebrates its centenary and try to realize the Chinese dream of great revival of the Chinese nation.	Remarks of Xi Jinping at the meeting with the National Model Workers on April 28, 2013
	Achieving the great rejuvenation of the Chinese nation is the greatest dream of the Chinese people in modern times and is the Chinese dream. The basic meaning is to achieve prosperity, revitalize the nation, and bring about the happiness of the people.	Remarks of Xi Jinping in Moscow Institute of International Relations on March 23, 2013
	More than 1.3 billion of Chinese people are dedicated to achieving the Chinese dream of the great revival of the Chinese nation while more than 1 billion African people are dedicated to the African dream of union, self-reliance, development and revitalization. The Chinese people and the African people shall strengthen solidarity, cooperation, mutual support and help to try to realize our respective dreams. We will work with the international community to promote the world dream of lasting peace and common prosperity and make new and greater contributions to the great cause of world peace and development!	Remarks of Xi Jinping at the Nyerere International Conference Center of Tanzania on March 25, 2013
	By the Chinese dream, we seek to have economic prosperity and national renewal and improve people's well-being. The Chinese dream is about cooperation, development, peace and win-win, and it is connected to the American Dream and the beautiful dreams people in other countries may have.	Remarks of Xi Jinping on June 7, 2013 when meeting reporters with President Obama

Rich Content of the Chinese Dream

Since elected secretary of the Central Committee of the CPC in 2012, Xi Jinping has explained the specific content, goals, general structure and paths for achieving the Chinese dream on different occasions at home and abroad. Immediately, the Chinese Dream has become even more popular and has richer meaning than the moderately prosperous society. The dream carries with it a long-cherished wish of generations of Chinese people. It reflects the interests of the Chinese people as a whole, and it's a common expectation of the Chinese nation.

On March 27, 2013, Xi Jinping pointed out in the keynote speech at the 5th BRICS Summit, "Everybody is concerned about the future development of China. Looking into the future, China will continuously march toward achievement of the two great goals: first is to double its 2010 GDP and per capita income for both urban and rural residents and built a moderately prosperous society that benefits a billion-plus Chinese people. The second is to turn China into a prosperous, strong, democratic and culturally advanced socialist country by 2049 when China celebrates its 100th anniversary of the founding of New China. To achieve these two great goals, we will continuously give priority to development, with economic development as the core task, and promote economic and social development. We will stick to putting people first and promote the economic, political, cultural, social and bio-civilization construction in an all-round way, and enhance coordinated development of modernization and build a beautiful China." Later, he pointed out again at the Bo'ao Forum for Asia on April 7, 2013, "The main goals we set for China are as follows: By 2020, China's GDP and per capita incomes for urban and rural residents will double the 2010 figures, and the building of a moderately prosperous society in all respects will be completed. By the mid-21st century, China will be turned into a modern socialist country that is prosperous, strong, democratic, culturally advanced and harmonious; and the Chinese dream, namely, the great renewal of the Chinese nation, will be realized.

The slogan of the Chinese dream in the streets of Beijing in December 2013.

We are aware that China remains the world's largest developing country, and it faces many difficulties and challenges on its road to progress. We need to make relentless efforts in the years ahead to deliver a better life to all our people. We are unwaveringly committed to reform and opening up, and we will concentrate on the major task of shifting the growth model, focus on running our own affairs well and make continued efforts to boost the socialist modernization drive."

The rich content of the Chinese Dream is reflected both in greater society and the smaller community. "The aspiration of the people to a life of well-being is our goal." On November 15, 2012, Xi Jinping made a speech of nearly 20 minutes at the news conference of the new Political Bureau of the Central Committee of the CPC. The focus of the speech was the people and the people's livelihood. For the common people, the speech was soul-stirring, "Our people love life and yearn for a better education, more stable employment, more satisfactory incomes, more reliable social security, better medical care services, more comfortable living conditions, and a more beautiful environment, and expect their children to grow better, have a better job and live a more comfortable life." The speech listed ten expectations of the common people, corresponding to the actual situation and the condition of people. Education, employment, income distribution, medical service, housing… have always been the keywords of the livelihood field and the focus of the social concerns and people's voice. From this sense, a series of livelihood development objectives in the report of the 18th National Congress of the CPC, and the "ten betters" put forward by Xi Jinping in his speech are active responses to the concerns of people's livelihoods, and specifically and clearly depict a picture of the future beautiful and happy lives for the people. This is also the beautiful vision outlined by the Chinese Dream for future social development.

Notes

1. Engel coefficient is an international comprehensive index measuring life quality and can objectively reflect the living status of people with different incomes and under different consumption price levels. According to the UN FAO's standard for living development stages, poverty exists when the Engel coefficient is above 60%, enjoying ample food and clothing supply when between 50–60%, enjoying relative prosperity when between 40–50%, in a state of affluence when between 30–40%, and experiencing high levels of affluence when below 30%. Currently, the Engel coefficient of the developed European and North American countries is normally around 20%.
2. However, due to the increase of urban poor in the wake of rising layoffs and unemployment, 19.98 million of the 320 million non-agricultural people had still been the urban poor by November, 2002. Therefore the government established the "Three Guarantee Lines" (basic living guarantee for laid-off workers from SOEs and unemployment insurance system and urban resident minimum subsistence allowances) to generally achieve the coverage of all those who qualified.
3. The 23 indices in six areas are: (1) Economic development: per capita GDP, percentage of R&D expenses in GDP, percentage of added value of tertiary industry in GDP, percentage of urban population, unemployment rate; (2) Social harmony: Gini coefficient, urban-rural residents' income comparison, coefficient for regional economic development difference, coverage of basic social insurance, coefficient for gender difference of high school graduates; (3) Life quality: per capita disposable income, Engel coefficient, per capita housing area, mortality of children under five, average life expectancy; (4) Democracy and legal system: citizen's satisfaction with democratic rights,

social security index; (5) Culture and education: percentage of cultural industry's added value in GDP, percentages of cultural, educational and recreational expenses in family's consumption, average education years; (6) Resources and environment: energy consumption per unit of GDP, agricultural acreage index, environmental quality index.

4. Emerging marketing countries, after breaking through the poverty trap with per capita GDP of $1,000, soon move to the takeoff stage with per capita GDP of $1,000–3,000. But when approaching per capita GDP of $3,000, the accumulated contradictions during the rapid development can suddenly become apparent. The system and mechanism upgrading reach critical points. When arriving at the stage, many developing countries, due to unconquerable economic development contradictions, faulty development strategies or external shocks, see declined or stagnant economy and fall into the so-called "middle-income trap."

New Circumstances and Challenges for Populous China

China is a populous country. According to World Bank statistics, in 2000, China ranked sixth in the world in terms of total GDP and 79th among 129 economies in terms of per capita GDP. In 2012, it ranked second in the world in terms of total GDP and 92nd among 180 economies in terms of per capita GDP. In the past 30 years, although China has shown the most stable growth of per capita GDP among the five BRICS countries, China still ranks the fourth among the five countries, only followed by India, which has the same problem caused by a rapid population increase. The population increase each year is equal to the population of a medium-sized country, consuming about 40% of the total GDP of the country and resulting in a low per capita GDP. At the same time, the floating population of China increased by about 6 million each year, while the aged population also increased by about 6 million each year. For China, there are three problems: low total increase rate but huge population base; insufficient economic development but huge number of aged population; limited urbanization but huge floating population. Those are three major trends of the development of the Chinese population since the beginning of the 21st century. In addition, imbalance in gender ratio of newborns is another headache, a challenge and a hidden trouble.

Fertility Policies and Population Increase

Basic Principle for Optimum Population

Perfect population structure and moderate population scale are the targets of modern societies. That's because everyone plays the roles of producer and consumer. As producers, people use means of production to become real productive forces; as consumers, naturally, people rely on enough means of subsistence (especially food) to meet their needs for reproduction. Therefore, employment and food supply are two major indicators for whether the population scale is moderate or not. Meanwhile, special attention should be paid to the environment and resources, which are closely related to the sustainability of employment and food supply. For example, if the food supply is insufficient and it is not due to unbalanced distribution or natural or man-made disasters, it is likely caused by a population increase that is faster than the increase of means of subsistence. Similarly, if underemployment is not caused by structural unemployment or an economic crisis, it should be caused by a population increase that is faster than the increase of means of production. These cases prove the existence of absolute surplus of population.Of course, population carrying capacity is a function of social productivity. Usually, in a closed society, adjustment of population scale and reduction of natural population growth rate are related more to fertility rate reduction or an increase in the mortality rate. It is shown that the mortality rate will fall as economic and social development improves. Thus, average life span will be longer, while the fertility rate will fall with increasing modernization. This indicates that when there is low-level modernization and an exceedingly rapid population increase, it is necessary for mankind to consciously influence the fertility rate. This is a common problem faced by developing economies. However, mankind did not realize this until the end of the 18th century, and it was not until the 19th and the mid-20th centuries that modern contraceptives were invented and popularized.

China's Population Increase and Fertility Policies

In terms of national territorial area, China ranks third among the countries in the world. Compared with Canada and the USA, which owned similar territorial area, China's population is 42 times larger than that of Canada, and 4.7 times larger than that of the USA. Compared with Russia, which has a larger territorial area, China's population is nine times larger than that of Russia. Generally, a country with a population of more than 50 million will be called

Today, people think more about marriage and future generations.

a populous country. However, the population of some Chinese provinces, such as Hebei, Shandong and Henan, exceeds 50 million. The Chinese people could stretch around the Earth's equator 50 times if they stood hand in hand.

Although China has been a populous country since ancient times, its rapid population increase only happened in the last half-century. Since its founding in 1949, the New China has seen a sharp rise in population, with several peaks. The first peak appeared in the early years of the New China, when chaos caused by wars had just subsided,good social order and fast economic development were maintained and medical and health conditions as well as the people's livelihood were greatly improved. In that case, the mortality rate fell sharply, and the "population explosion" that had happened in many countries after the World War II also occurred in China. On November 1, 1954, the Chinese government published the results of the first national population census. The bulletin indicated that, by 24:00 on June 30, 1953, the total population of China had reached 582.6 million, over 100 million more than the 475 million estimated when the New China was founded. The data led to various public opinions and wide discussion about whether birth control should be implemented. Finally, the opinions embracing moderate birth control prevailed. These opinions said, the more children a family has, the more burdens for the parents, family and even the children themselves, such as insufficient supply of clothing, food, medical care and schooling, which might be hard to solve at all once. Therefore, the government made policies on family planning. Then, after experiencing an abnormal three-year negative population increase at the end of the 1950s and the beginning of the 1960s, the second "population explosion" appeared with stronger momentum. The newborn population in 1962 was equal to the total newborn population in the previous two years combined. There were even more newborns in 1963, the year with the most newborns and the highest birth rate and natural increase rate since the founding of the New China. This, again, caught the attention of the Chinese government leaders. Marked by the issue of the Instructions on Promoting Family Planning by the Central Committee of the CPC

A traditional big family in China.

and the State Council at the end of 1962, family planning in China, especially in urban areas, entered a new stage. At the beginning of 1964, the Family Planning Committee and the Family Planning Office of the State Council were established to enhance guidance and coordination for family planning programs and provide greater financial support for related work, including research, development and production of contraceptives. At the beginning of the 1970s, to cope with the high fertility rate and natural population increase rate, the family planning program was included in the national economic plan. The State Council established the Family Planning Leading Group to extend family planning policies to all the urban and rural areas of China. The population increase rate gradually slowed, and the net population increase decreased from more than 19.5 million in 1971 to 11 million in 1977 (decreasing by 31 million within six years), with the natural increase rate declining by 11.3% and the annual average increase lower than that in the 1960s and 1950s. It's worth noting that during this period greater efforts were made via local administrative intervention for the implementation of family

The rate of the growth of China's population has been effectively reduced due to family planning policy.

planning policies, though the central government continued to adhere to the principle of focus on dissemination of information, rely on the masses and avoid coercion.

The return of educated youth to the urban areas at the end of the 1970s5 promoted the issue of policies on self-employment and multiple channels for solving problems concerning employment. In rural areas, various responsibility systems for agricultural production gradually replaced the collective working schemes under the system of people's communes. This raised the curtain of the reform and opening-up of China in the modern era, and, to some extent, released the pressure on population that used to come from traditional systems. In the face of the conflict between population increase and resources, employment and economic development, the Chinese government was forced to adjust the family planning policy to call for "late marriage, longer birth spacing and fewer

Table 2-1-1
General Data of the Six National Population Census

Indicators	1953	1964	1982	1990	2000	2010
Total population (ten thousand people)	58260	69458	100818	113368	126583	133972
Gender ratio (based on 100 females)	107.56	105.46	106.30	106.60	106.74	105.20
Family size (member(s)/household)	4.33	4.43	4.41	3.96	3.44	3.10
Proportion by age (%)						
0-14 years old	36.28	40.69	33.59	27.69	22.89	16.60
15-64 years old	59.31	55.75	61.50	66.74	70.15	74.53
65 and above	4.41	3.56	4.91	5.57	6.96	8.87
Population by nationality						
The Han nationality (ten thousand people and proportion %)	54728 (93.94)	65456 (94.24)	94088 (93.32)	104248 (91.96)	115940 (91.59)	122593 (91.51)
People of ethnic groups (ten thousand people and proportion %)	3532 (6.06)	4002 (5.76)	6730 (6.68)	9120 (8.04)	10643 (8.41)	11379 (8.49)
Different groups by education of each 100,000 people (member)						
Junior college degree and above		416	615	1422	3611	8930
Senior high school and secondary technical school		1319	6779	8039	11146	14032
Junior high school		4680	17892	23344	33961	38788
Primary school		28330	35237	37057	35701	26779
Illiterate population (ten thousand people and proportion %)		23327 (33.58)	22996 (22.81)	18003 (15.88)	8507 (6.72)	5466 (4.08)

Urban and rural population (ten thousand people)						
Urbanization rate %	13.26	18.30	20.91	26.44	36.22	49.68
Urban population	7726	12710	21082	29971	45844	66557
Rural population	50534	56748	79736	83397	80739	67415
Average life expectancy (years)			67.77*	68.55	71.40	74.83
Females			66.28*	66.84	69.63	72.38
Males			69.27*	70.47	73.33	77.37

Notes:

1. The standard starting time for the national population censuses in 1953, 1964, 1982 and 1990 was 0:00am on July 1, while that for the national population censuses in 2000 and 2010 was 0:00am on November 1.
2. Each census covered military personnel of the Chinese People's Liberation Army in active service, which were considered urban population.
3. The illiterate population in 1964 referred to people 13 and older who were illiterate, while the illiterate population in 1982, 1990, 2000 and 2010 included people 15 and older who were illiterate or could read a little.
4. "*" means data obtained in 1981.

Data source: *China Statistical Yearbook (2012)*, National Bureau of Statistics.

children". In 1980, the Chinese government formally issued the one-child policy, mandating that a couple should just have one child. In 1981, the National Family Planning Commission was established as an independent department of the State Council. Since 1982, the family planning policy has been deemed as a basic state policy carried out by enforcement. In addition, the functions of both the central and local family planning departments have been enhanced in the process of restructuring of government administration to guarantee the implementation of the family planning policies. The *Instructions of the Central Committee of the CPC and the State Council on Further Promoting Family* Planning issued early this year specified the strategic significance of family planning: "It is a major task of China to figure out how to keep the population increase in line with national

Family is the cornerstone of the Chinese society.

economic development… there are two possibilities in front of us: put strict and effective control on population increase to improve all the people's lives and gradually expand nation-building or allow the population to greatly increase, which will be an obstacle for improvement of all the people's lives and the economic, cultural and national defense construction." In 1982, both the report of the 12th National Congress of the CPC and the newly amended Constitution spoke favorably of the family planning policy.

After 1982, to guarantee implementation of the one-child policy, some necessary adjustments were made based upon the experiences of local governments. The first was to relax the restrictions on giving birth to a second child (especially in rural areas).The second was to strictly prohibit unplanned birth. The third was to set clear policies on family planning of ethnic groups. The fourth was to reform the family planning programs concerning the floating population and such programs in urban areas. Since 1991, the Central Committee of the CPC has held meetings and symposiums on population and family planning programs nearly every year. In 2001, the *Population and Family Planning Law of the People's Republic of China* was issued to further consolidate the status of the family planning policy as a basic state policy by law, putting an end to the history that population and family planning programs were carried out just based on policies and local regulations, stabilizing the fertility policies and integrating family planning into the legal system.

Therefore, from the 1970s to the 1990s, China completed its transformation of the population reproduction pattern, namely from high birth rate, low mortality rate and high growth rate to low birth rate, low mortality rate and low growth rate. The total fertility rate approached the replacement level6. Figure 2-1-1 shows that, during this period, China had a relatively stable mortality rate, and natural population increase rate was highly consistent with the birth rate. In the 1980s, when the third peak of population increase occurred, there were two fluctuations. From 1981 to 1990, the birth rate had been above 20‰, while the natural increase rate ranged from 13.08‰ to 16.61‰, and the population increased by more than 15 million each year. Entering the 1990s, both birth rate and increase rate had been declining. The birth rate had declined from 19.68‰ in 1991 to 14.03‰ in 2000, while the natural increase rate had declined from 12.98‰ to 7.58‰, and the population increase of each year reduced by about 2

Stamps of family planning with a set of two, issued in September 1983.

"Adhere to administration according to law, and work for harmonious family planning." A slogan of family planning of Beisheng Village in the Ancheng Town, Pingyin County, Shangdong Province on July 6th, 2013.

million compared with that in the 1980s. Since the beginning of the 21st century, the birth rate has declined to 11.9‰ to 13.38‰, while the natural increase rate has been in the single digits, showing a gradual slowdown of population increase, with a population increase of more than 7 million each year. In the future, the natural increase rate of the Chinese population will continue to fall, and the annual population increase will continue to slow. However, this will be a gradual process. As estimated, it may take more than 20 years to have zero or even negative population growth, with a peak of about 1.5 million. Before that, the China, the current No.1 most populous country in the world, will be caught up by India in terms of population size, and will become the No.2 most populous country in the world.

Figure 2-1-1
Chinese Population Growth, 1978–2011

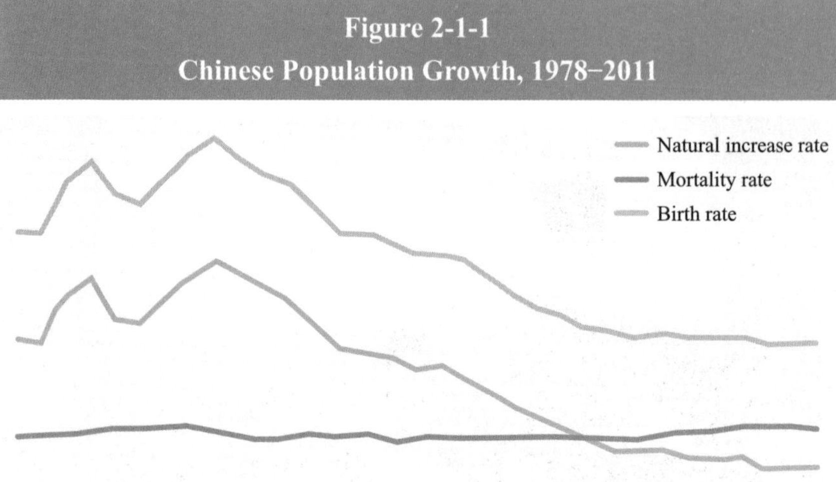

1978 1981 1983 1985 1987 1989 1991 1993 1995 1997 1999 2001 2003 2005 2007 2009 2011

Data source: *China Statistical Yearbook* (2012).

Positive Effects of the Family Planning Policy

When discussing the brilliant achievements since the reform and opening-up of China, the positive effects of family planning policy should be mentioned. On one hand, during this time, China enjoyed a large working population, relatively low dependency ratio, the ability to provide low-cost labor resources and a high savings rate. Under the guarantees of a good economic system, those became the sources and motivation for fast economic growth. On the other hand, sustainable implementation of the family planning policy not only relieved the economic and resource burdens, but also provided great potential for improvement and development of human capital. The table (Table 2-1-2) in the geography textbook of junior middle school students indicated the values of family planning and lower population increase rate. The *China Sustainable Development Strategy Report 2000* released by the Chinese Academy of Sciences said that the GDP consumption of the increased population each year had declined from 25% in 1980s to 18% in 1999, with an average annual declining rate of nearly one percentage point. This proves the great success of the population policies. The report also said that realization of the strategic target of China for zero population growth will drive a GDP increase of 1.2 to 1.5 percentage points annually, cause new jobs to increase by a factor of 0.065 to 0.07 each year, make the falling rate of the elasticity coefficient of resources and energy utilization speed up by a factor of 0.02, guarantee that the national average education years will reach 12 years by 2050, accelerate an increase of average life expectancy by a factor of 0.15 and speed up an increase of the cultural development index by a factor of 0.13. No matter how controversial these data were, it's true that, for many years, China has been maintaining a GDP growth rate higher than the global average, while its per capita GDP is lower than the global average.

The population structure of China indicates a huge proportion of working age population and sufficient labor resources. In 2010, there were 940 million people aged from 15 to 59, accounting for 70% of the total population. The working-age population reached its peak during the 12th Five-Year Plan and then began to fall. However, the working-age population will still remain at more than 800 million, more than the total population of Europe. Therefore, China will not lack labor forces in the future and it will be a long-term task for full employment. Since reform and opening-up, China has been relying on abundant,

Table 2-1-2
Natural Resources of China

Population	World Ranking by Natural Resource	World Ranking by Per Capita Availability
1.295 billion (middle of 2004)	4th by agricultural acreage	67th
	6th by forestry area	121st
	3rd by annual output of ore	80th
	6th by total water resource	88th

low-cost labor resources to participate in the international division of labor and gradually become a big manufacturing country. Today the added value of the Chinese manufacturing sector accounts for about 20% of that of the world manufacturing sector. In terms of this, China has caught up with the USA and ranks the top in the world. As a developing populous country, China needs the support of the manufacturing sector to fulfill strategic targets set for the middle of the 21st century. However, generally, the Chinese manufacturing sector is at the low end of the value chain, with low industrial added value. Therefore, under such a circumstance that many large economies are engaging in "returning to strategy to develop the real economy", it is an urgent need to move up the

Figure 2-1-2
Proportion of Consumption of Increased Population of Each Year of the Newly Added Wealth of the Year

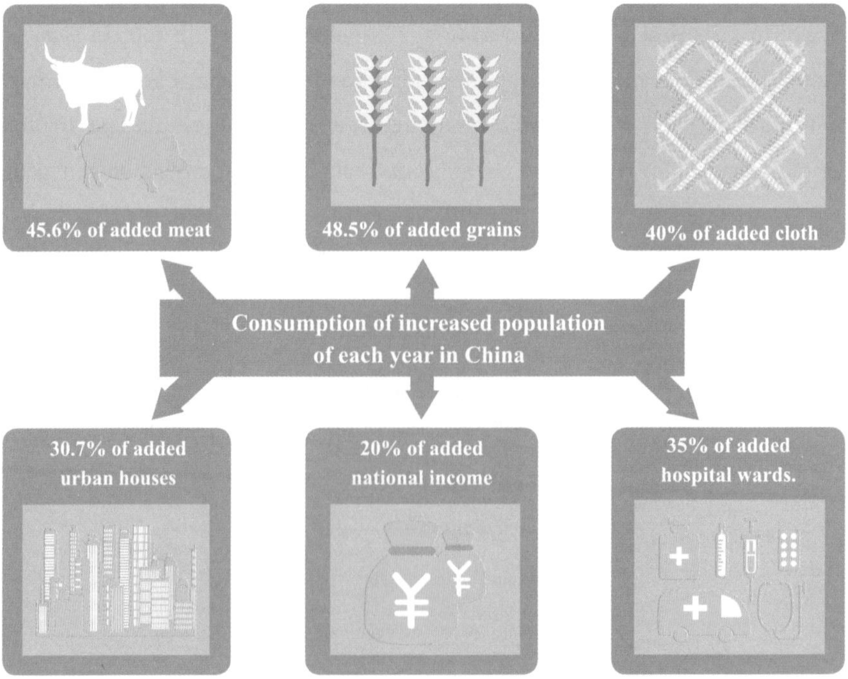

45.6% of added meat

48.5% of added grains

40% of added cloth

Consumption of increased population of each year in China

30.7% of added urban houses

20% of added national income

35% of added hospital wards.

China boasts rich labor resources.

industrial chain. In addition, there is great surplus production capacity in the Chinese manufacturing sector. Therefore, the only way to solve the problem is industrial restructuring and changing the development mode, for which the global economic crisis in recent years served as a driving force and provided a great opportunity. The economic upgrade of China should rely on technological development, improvement of labor productivity and effective human resource structure. In China, the improvement of the skills of the population and the construction of a powerful country with an effective human resource structure have become the key elements for improving core competitiveness and ensuring sustainable economic growth.

Downsizing of Families and Aging of Population

Change of Dependency Ratio of Population and Family Size

Figure 2-2-1 indicates the change of dependency ratio of the Chinese population based on the data of the sixth population census. Since the implementation of the compulsory family planning policy, population growth has slowed, while the population age structure has quickly changed. In accordance with the sixth population census, the dependency ratio of population declined, from 79.4 (the peak) in 1964 and 62.6 in 1982, and then to 49.8 in 1990, 42.6 in 2000 and 43.2 in 2010. The huge amount of saved dependency expenditure became the so called "demographic dividend". However, Table 2-2-1 indicates that when fertility rates fell greatly, there was a fall of children dependency ratio and an increase of old-age dependency ratio, though the dependency ratio of the total population had a decline. In addition, with the fall of the total fertility rate of women, there was a decrease of family sizes. The average family

Table 2-2-1
Family Sizes and Total Fertility Rates Based on the Data of the Six Population Census

Indicator	1953	1964	1982	1990	2000	2010
Family size (member(s)/household)	4.33	4.43	4.41	3.96	3.44	3.1
Total fertility rate	6.05	6.18	2.86	2.31	1.23	1.18

Data source: *China Population and Employment Statistics Yearbook 2007*; *Data of the Fifth Population Census*; *Data of China's Population Census in 2010.*

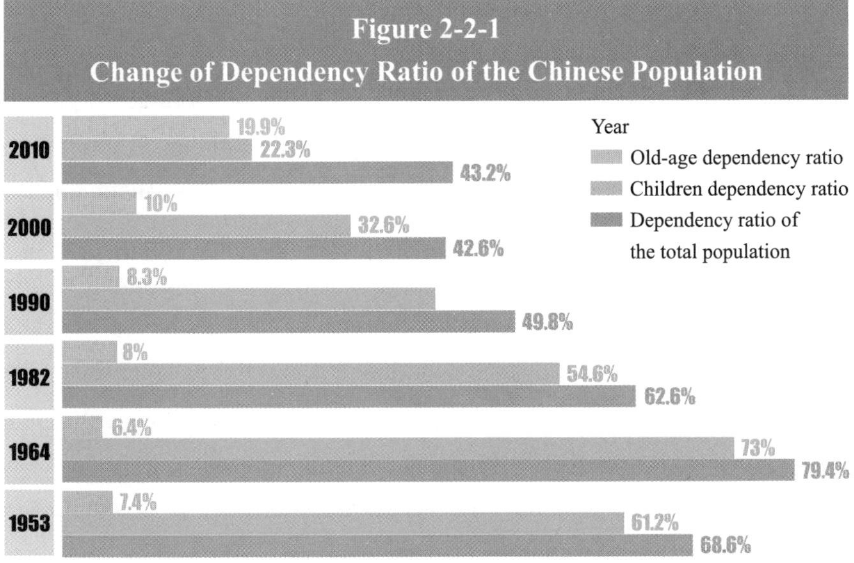

Figure 2-2-1
Change of Dependency Ratio of the Chinese Population

members reduced from 4.41 in 1982 to 3.96, 3.44 and 3.1 in 1990, 2000 and 2010, respectively. The experiences of developed countries shows that, with increasingly improved industrialization and urbanization, population mobility has been enhanced. Therefore, the downsizing of Chinese families will continue in the future. Such a tendency has caused the change of functions of families, especially weakening the ability to take care of the elderly.

Downsizing of Families

By intergenerational structure and relationship, families are divided into the following categories: (1) nuclear family consisting of parents and their unmarried children; (2) stem family, a type of extended family, which consists of parents and one child and his or her spouse, for example, the parents and their son and their son's wife; (3) joint family, also called composite family, a type of extended family composed of parents, their children, and the children's spouses and offspring in one household; (4) other types of families. The downsizing of families is proved by the increased proportion of nuclear families. There are several reasons. First, traditionally, China has been a big country inclining to agricultural development with the small-scale peasant economy playing a dominant role so that nuclear families have been taking a large proportion of the Chinese families, and the tendency of nuclear families in rural areas were promoted by the agricultural collectivization and the household contract and management system. Second, with a wider range of industrialization, marketization and urbanization as well as the extension of modern way of life, which led to larger-scale population flow, change of concepts on marriage and family7, increased cost of education and low fertility desire, the tendency for nuclear families has been enhanced. Third, to some extent, the family planning policy promoted the increase of single-child families, especially in urban areas (single-child families accounted for more than 50% of the city's families in Beijing, Shanghai and Tianjin), which were more strictly limited by the policy. Meanwhile, for these reasons, the dominant status of the nuclear families in the family structure of China has been enhanced and highlighted.

Today, a Chinese family usually has three people, the parents and a child.

Table 2-2-2 Family Structure Under Three Population Census				
Time of Census		1982	1990	2000
Nuclear family	A Couple	4.78	6.49	12.93
	Parents and children	52.89	57.81	47.52
	One parent and children	14.31	9.50	6.35
	Expanded			1.62
	Total	71.98	73.80	68.15
Stem family	Two generations			2.37
	Three generations	16.63	16.65	16.63
	Four generations	0.52	0.59	0.64
	Generation-skipping	0.66	0.66	2.09
	Total	17.81	17.90	21.73
Joint family	Two generations	0.11	0.09	0.13
	More than three generations	0.88	1.06	0.44
	Total	0.99	1.15	0.57
One-member family		7.97	6.32	8.57
Single-parent family				0.73
Other		1.02	0.81	0.26
Total		100.00	100.00	100.00

Data source: Analysis on Change of Contemporary Chinese Family Structure, by Wang Yuesheng, Social Science in China, First Issue, 2006.

Continuous growth in the proportion of nuclear families was a major trend in Chinese families in the latter half of the 20th century, keeping in line with the general tendency of industrialization and urbanization. However, as shown in Table 2-2-2, the proportion of nuclear families declined in 2000 compared with 1990. Some scholars believe this should be directly related to the significant fall of birth rate in rural areas since the 1970s.8 Some scholars also point out that it's because the number of stem families had an increase due to the sharp decrease of multiple-child families9 and the unsound pension security system in rural areas. The data of the population census in 2010 further proved such a tendency. In terms of the family scales, compared with 2000, the three-member families decreased from 29.95% to 26.86%, while the two-member families and one-member families respectively increased from 17.04% to 24.37%, and from 8.30% to 14.53%; in total, the one-member, two member and three-member families had an increase of 10.47 percentage points; the families with four members and above decreased. This indicated an obvious downsizing trend.

While the proportion of joint families decreased and the proportion of nuclear families decreased slightly, the proportions of two-member families and one-member families rose. This probably indicates an increase of one-couple families, single-parent families and families with member(s) living alone10. The one-couple families may include DINK families and even empty-nest families and families with the only child lost. Families with member(s) living alone may include single-person families (including those divorced) and even the widowed-spouse families. The increase of empty-nest families and widowed-spouse families, especially the inclination of the nuclear families toward empty-nest families, is a product of the downsizing of families and the aging of population.

Aging of Population

With a lower fertility rate and a longer life expectancy, in accordance with international standards, China has moved toward becoming an aging society since the end of the 20th century and the beginning of the 21st century. It is one of the earliest developing countries to become an aging society.11 With a large population base, longer life expectancy12 and accelerated aging process, China will soon become the country with the most aged population in the world. As predicted by the UN, from 1990 to 2020, the average growth rate of the aged population of the whole world was 2.5%, while the growth rate of the aged population of China during the same period was 3.3%; the proportion of the aged population to the total population of the world increased from 6.6% in 1995 to 9.3% in 2020, while the proportion of the aged population to the total population of the country increased from 6.1% to 11.5%. This indicates that China has a faster-growing aged population as well as proportion of the aged population to the total population than the world average. By 2020, China will have 167 million aged people over 65, accounting for 24% of the world's aged population, which will reach 698 million. There will be one Chinese elderly person out of every four elderly people in the world. There is a general indicator for measuring the speed of the aging of population, namely the time for the proportion of the population aged 65 and above to increase from 7% to 14% and then to 21%. As shown in Figure 2-2-2, many developed countries saw slow aging of their populations. For example, in France, it took more than 100 years for the proportion of the population aged 65 and above to rise from 7% to 14%,

China has come to an aging society.

Figure 2-2-2
Time for Proportion of Population Aged 65 and Above in Selected Countries to Raise from 7% to 14% and Then to 21%

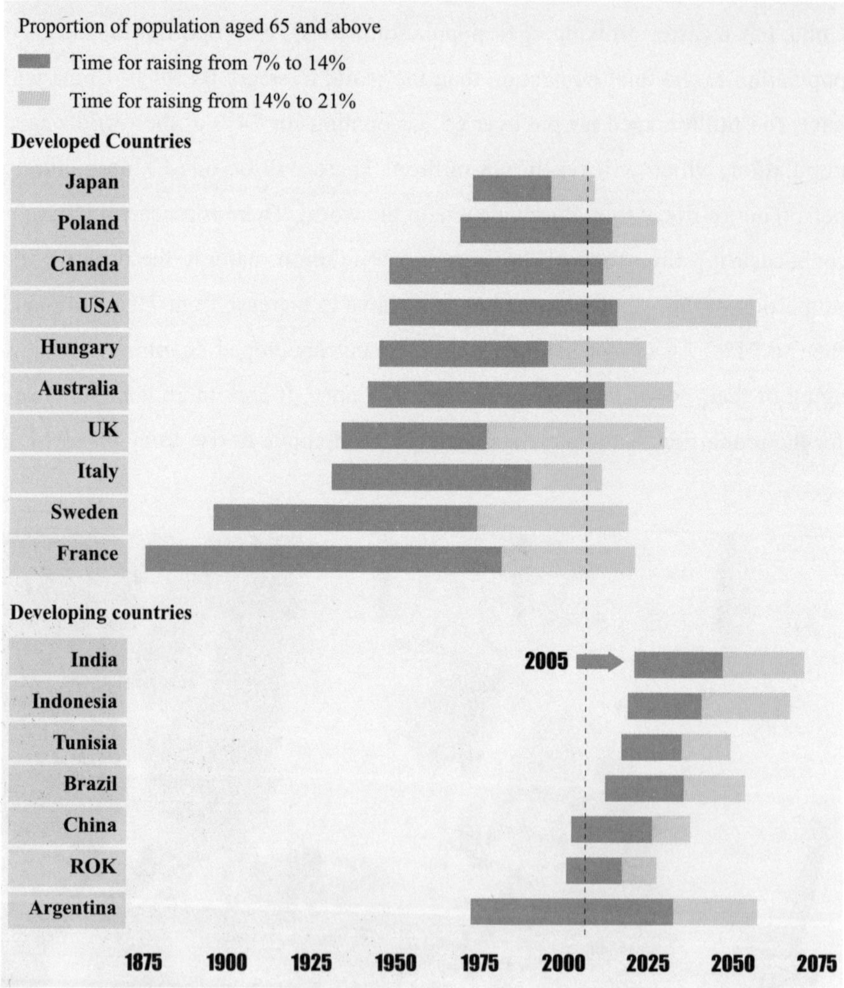

Proportion of population aged 65 and above
Time for raising from 7% to 14%
Time for raising from 14% to 21%

Developed Countries

Japan
Poland
Canada
USA
Hungary
Australia
UK
Italy
Sweden
France

Developing countries

India
Indonesia
Tunisia
Brazil
China
ROK
Argentina

2005

1875 1900 1925 1950 1975 2000 2025 2050 2075

Data source: *World Economic and Social Survey 2007: Development in an Ageing World*, UN Department of Economic and Social Affairs, P13, www.un.org.

and it was predicted that it will take another 40 years for this proportion to reach 21%. Compared with that, it may only take 40 years for such proportion of Japan to rise from 7% to 21%. However, many developing countries including China, ROK and Tunisia have seen a fast aging of their populations. This is because these countries have experienced a fast decrease of fertility rate. In addition, in many countries, the increase of population aged 80 and above is faster than that of the elderly population at other ages. It indicates the gradual aging of the structure of the aged population.

Figure 2-2-3 shows the predictions for the aging of the Chinese population in the first half of the 21st century made in the report of the National Population Development Strategic Research Group of the original State Family Planning Commission in 2007. It was predicted that by 2020, the proportion of population aged above 60 and that of population aged above 65 may reach 16.0% and 11.2%, and may reach 30% and 22% in the later 2040s. The report said that unsound rural social pension security system and migration of a great number of young laborers to cities caused more serious aging of population in rural areas.

Experience of developed countries indicates that the aging of population structure is an irreversible tendency, but its consequences depend on the policies made to overcome the challenges. For most societies, the aging of population may result in decrease of working population with income relative to population not working and relying on others' income, and increase of the dependency ratio of aged population and even the increase of the overall social dependency ratio. In many developed countries, the dependency ratio of populations reached their lowest points in 2005. Considering continuous increase of the dependency ratio of the aged population, it is predicted that the dependency ratio of the overall population of the developed countries may have a gradual increase. The tendency of China is strikingly similar to that of the developed countries, though China is still a developing country. Figure 2-2-4 indicates the tendency of the dependency ratio of China predicted by the UN. The data indicates that, compared with that

Figure 2-2-3
Predicted Tendency of the Aging of Population in China

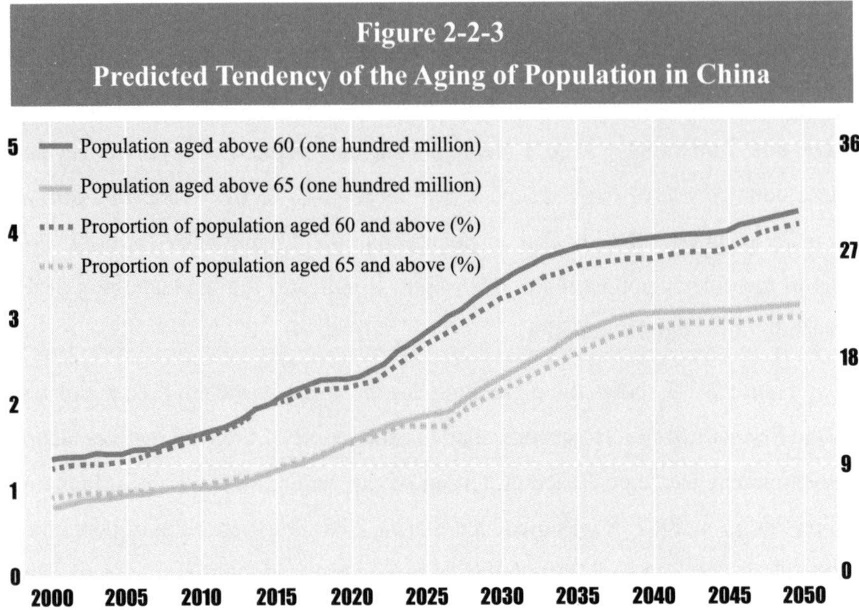

Data source: *Research Report on National Population Development Strategy,* 2007, www.gov.cn , January 11, 2007.

Figure 2-2-4
Change of Dependency Ratio of China Predicted by the UN

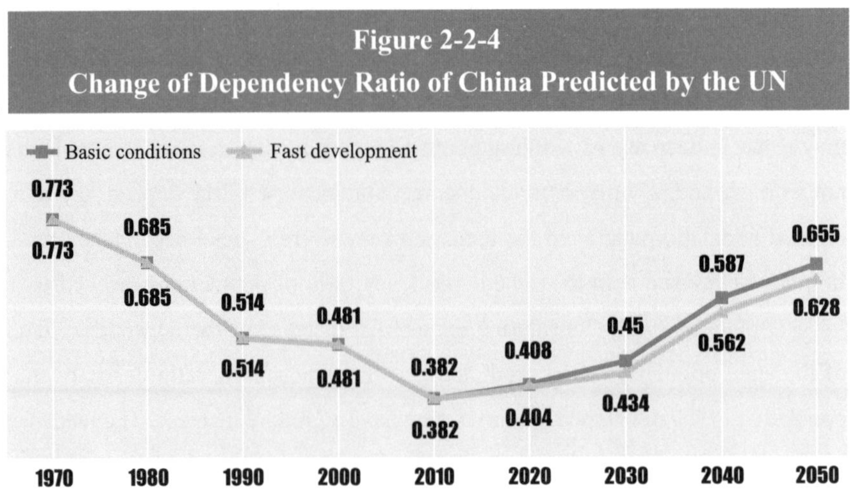

Data source: *2013 Human Development Report*, United Nations Development Porgramme, P99. The overlaps of the two lines mean actual tendency, while the separated parts mean predicted tendency.

of the developed countries, it took the dependency ratio of China five more years to reach the lowest point; after 2010, with the increase of the dependency ratio of the aged population, the overall social dependency ratio had an increase, By 2035, it will be recovered to the level of 1990; by 2050, it will approach the level of 1980, but with a reversal of the dependency ratios of children and the elderly.

Empty-nest Families and Weakened Function of Families for Elderly Care

In the developing countries, most of the elderly live together with their children. In Asia and Africa, 3/4 of the elderly aged 60 or above live with their children; in Latin America, 2/3 of the elderly live with their children. Only a small number of the elderly live alone. China has the tradition of "rearing sons to support parents in their old age". Even today, there are still 60% of the elderly in rural areas (including those with children who worked outside hometown) and about 50% of the elderly in urban areas living with their children. Family-based elderly care has been the norm in China. In rural areas, since there is no formal retirement system and social security mechanism, the children are usually responsible for taking care of their parents after they lose the ability to work. The constitution of the People's Republic of China stipulates that adult offspring have the obligation to provide for their parents. The *Marriage Law of the People's Republic of China* stipulates that parents shall have the obligations to bring up and educate their children while children shall have the obligations to support and assist their parents. The *Law of the People's Republic of China on Protection of the Rights and Interests of the Elderly* stipulates, "the elderly shall be provided for mainly by their families, and their family members shall care for and look after them," and "supporters of the elderly shall perform the duties of providing for the elderly, taking care of them and comforting them, and cater to their special needs."

However, this elderly care system is being increasingly impacted by the trends of family downsizing and aging of population. Only-child families have

Family Structure of China

Cartoon: How to afford a family in form of "4+2+1"?

a structure consisting of four parents, a young couple and one child. The young couple may shoulder heavy duties. Therefore, many parents choose to, or have to, live alone, resulting in the phenomenon of the"empty nest". In the 1980s, only 10% of families with elderly members were empty-nest families. Ten years later, it increased to 30%. In 2000, based on the results of the fifth national population census, the families with elderly aged 65 or above accounted for 20.09% (1/5) of the families of the country, while the empty-nest families accounted for 22.83%, and empty-nest families with a single old man or woman accounted for 11.46%. In 2012, the empty-nest families accounted for nearly 49.7% of the families with the elderly; meanwhile, the empty-nest families in rural areas experienced a rapid increase of 38.3%.

The only-child family structure makes the empty-nest period come earlier and last longer. Family-based elderly care is based on a fragile foundation with a number of problems concerning financial resources, daily care, communication with children and spiritual consolation. The parents usually get limited support from their children. One of the major influences of the only-child policy is the weakened foundation of the "family culture" that had been embraced in the traditional society. In many aspects, the experience of the Chinese people in elderly care accumulated based on the family structure with more than one child cannot provide reference for the elderly care of the only-child families.

Of the empty-nest families, those with the only child lost attract more attention. In accordance with the *China Health Statistical Yearbook (2010)* of the Ministry of Health, there are 76,000 more families with the only child lost each year, and such families with the elderly aged 50 and above are increasing.So far, there have been more than one million families with the only child lost. Some experts estimated that, from 1975 to 2010, a total 218 million babies were born in only-child families, however, more than 10 million of which died before they were 25 years old. It means that 20 million people lost their only one child and had to live alone.

Large-scale Population Flow and Migration

Large-scale population flow of rural migrant workers

In China, whenever population flow is referred to, what's most impressive should be the great number of rural migrant workers that continuously flow into cities, and the Spring Festival Travel, which is a special Chinese term meaning transportation during the Spring Festival holiday. Like the West's Christmas, the Spring Festival holiday is an important holiday for the Chinese people to spend time with their family members. Therefore, during the holiday, all the railway stations, long-distance bus stations, airports and ports are full of people. It is really a spectacular phenomenon, and even an incredible phenomenon to the rest of the world. During the last Spring Festival Travel period, which lasted for 40 days, there were 3.6 billion travels throughout the country, more than the total journeys of the country throughout the whole year of 2013. These years, the Chinese tourist market has experienced prosperous development. The statistics of the National Bureau of Statistics indicate that, in 2013, Chinese tourists made 3.26 billion domestic journeys and 98.19 million outbound journeys (including 91.97 million due to private reasons), each with an increase of 10.3% and 18% over the previous year (an increase of travel due to private reasons of 19.3%), and respectively 3.7 and 3.4 times as much as those in 2003 (6.2 times for travels due to private reasons). However, the population flow mentioned here does not include activities due to business travel, need for medical care, attending school, travel, and visits to relatives and friends, since people concerned with these activities will go back to the places where their household registrations were made within some time. The floating population mentioned here mainly includes

Chang'an Bus Station in Dongguan City, Guangdong Province. Migrant workers coming back home by coach crowded into the bus station during the Spring Festival travel season.

The majority of the floating people in China are the farmers who seek jobs in cities.

rural migrant workers, "drifters in Beijing"13 and other adults and people at childbearing age who work and live in places outside their hometowns where their household registrations were made.

Since the reform and opening-up policies were put into practice, wide-range population flow has taken off. China is now at a stage for increasingly accelerated urbanization. So far, the population flow is following a trend from rural areas to urban areas and from the central and western parts of China to the southeastern coastal areas. The 1 % sampling survey made in 2005 indicated that, a total floating population of 147.35 million was distributed all over the country. Concerning proportion of floating population to local total population, Henan province ranked the last with a proportion of 2.52%. Some cities and economically developed areas are major destinations of the floating population. For example, the proportion of the floating population to local total population of Shanghai, Guangdong, Beijing, Zhejiang and Fujian respectively reached 34%, 26%, 23%, 20% and 19%, or, one of every five or even three people are

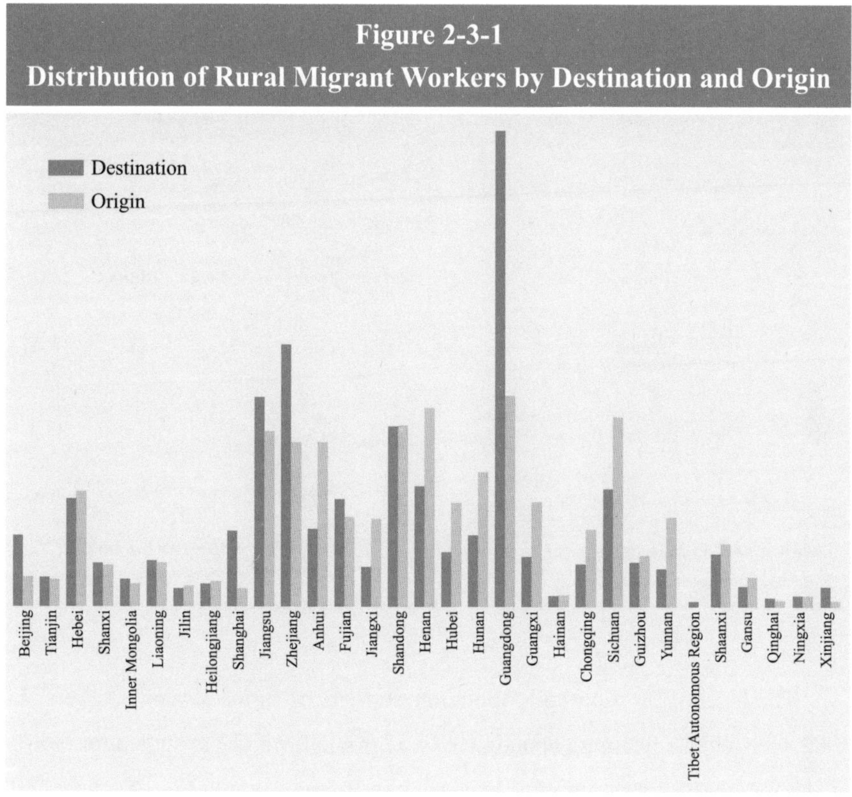

Figure 2-3-1
Distribution of Rural Migrant Workers by Destination and Origin

Data source: The *2012 Survey and Monitoring Report on Chinese Rural Migrant Worker*, National Bureau of Statistics.

a member of the floating population. By comparing the results of the sixth population census made in 2010 with that of the fifth population census, the proportion of the local total population of Guangzhou to the national population increased from 6.83% to 7.79%, exceeding 100 million; that of Beijing increased from 1.09% to 1.46%; that of Tianjin increased from 0.79% to 0.97%; that of Shanghai increased from 1.32% to 1.72%; that of Zhejiang increased from 3.69% to 4.06%. A large part of the increased population came from the floating population.

Table 2-3-1
Number of Rural Migrant Workers From 2008 to 2012 by 10,000 People

	2008	2009	2010	2011	2012
Total number of rural migrant workers	22542	22978	24223	25278	26261
1. Outbound rural migrant workers	14041	14533	15335	15863	16336
(1). Rural migrant workers under household survey	11182	11567	12264	12584	12961
(2). Rural migrant workers migrating with families	2859	2966	3071	3279	3375
2. Local rural migrant workers	8501	8445	8888	9415	9925

Data source: The 2012 *Survey and Monitoring Report on Chinese Rural Migrant Workers*, National Bureau of Statistics.

The bulk of the floating population consists of rural migrant workers. In 1982, China had a floating population of 6.57 million, which accounted for 0.66% of the national total population.In 1987, the floating population reached 18.1 million.In 1995, it reached 70.73 million, accounting for 5.86% of the national total. In 2000, it made a breakthrough of 100 million. In 2005, China had a floating population of 147 million , accounting for 11.3% of the national total population. Of them, about 120 million people (nearly 80%) were rural migrant workers working outside their hometowns. In 2009, the floating population reached about 180 million, including 149 million (more than 80%) rural migrant workers working outside their hometowns. In 2010, the floating population reached 221 million, while the number of rural migrant workers reached 242 million, including 153 million working outside hometown. In 2011, the floating population reached 230 million, accounting for 17% of national total population, including 159 million rural migrant workers working outside their hometowns. In 2012, the floating population reached 236 million (meaning one of every six

The wealthy countryside in the east coastal areas of China.

Chinese people was a member of the floating population), including 163 million rural migrant workers working outside their hometowns. In recent years, there has been a reduction of rural migrant workers working in other provinces other than the one they were born in. However, the floating population still accounts for about 70% of the total population.

Transfer of Surplus Agricultural Labor Force and the "Dual Structure"

The rural migrant workers are a main part of the floating population. Where do they come from? Since ancient times, China has traditionally had a small-scale peasant economy, with men farming and women weaving. Such tradition allows the farmers to make extra earnings for their families by doing business other than farming. At the beginning of the reform and opening-up of China, such tradition was recovered and developed. However, along with industrial and commercial development as well as the change of industrial and economic structures, especially the obvious improvement of agricultural labor productivity and increase of surplus agricultural laborers, and limited by the per

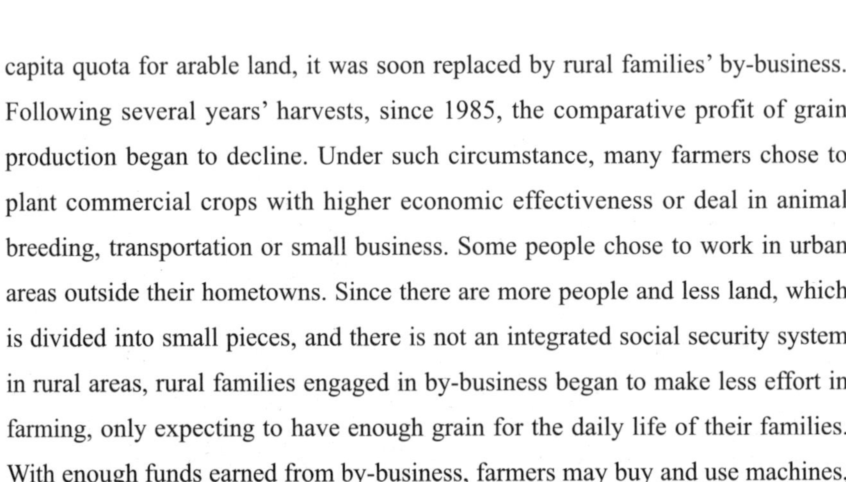

capita quota for arable land, it was soon replaced by rural families' by-business. Following several years' harvests, since 1985, the comparative profit of grain production began to decline. Under such circumstance, many farmers chose to plant commercial crops with higher economic effectiveness or deal in animal breeding, transportation or small business. Some people chose to work in urban areas outside their hometowns. Since there are more people and less land, which is divided into small pieces, and there is not an integrated social security system in rural areas, rural families engaged in by-business began to make less effort in farming, only expecting to have enough grain for the daily life of their families. With enough funds earned from by-business, farmers may buy and use machines, chemical fertilizers and pesticides or hire others to do farming, or even lease their contracted farmland to others while buying grain from the market. With increased employment opportunities from the industrial sector and the service industry, for many rural families with by-business, farming has become a sideline.

From an overall perspective, the phenomenon mentioned above does not mean that all the labor in a rural family is focused on by-business. For families with enough land and few opportunities for seeking outside employment, all the members of the family may be engaged in farming, and they may even need to hire others to help them during busy seasons. However, for most rural families, which have less farmland (about 1.3 *mu* per capita) that the elderly and women can manage to till, young laborers may seek job opportunities in cities or engage in transportation or small businesses to earn extra money for their families. At the very beginning, the non-agricultural activities were just intermittent activities during slack seasons. However, later, young laborers become rural migrant workers, who do not come back to farm even in the busy seasons. In that case, farming becomes the responsibility of the elderly, women and kids. Sometimes, other people are hired to help them, or the farmland is leased to others. Some farmland may even be abandoned. Relevant surveys indicated that, regarding disposal of contracted farmland of rural migrant workers, 63.86% of respondents said that the other members of their families would take care of the farmland;

20.98% of said the farmland had been leased to relatives and friends; 8.03% of said that the farmland has been abandoned; and 7.13% of people mentioned other disposal methods, including returning farmland to forests or grassland.

However, it's not easy for farmers to completely abandon their contracted farmland. It is a decision that should be made by all the family members, not just by the members who are migrant workers. Outside employment may be not stable. For example, several years ago, impacted by global economic crisis, thousands of rural migrant workers lost their jobs and had to return home. In that case, it was lucky for them that they had farmland. In fact, instability and frequent turnover are very common problems for rural migrant workers. It is not common for rural migrant workers to get jobs through government departments and labor intermediaries. Most of these people got a job by themselves or by the recommendation of their relatives and friends. They may not sign employment contracts with their employers. They are not well-educated and get little chances for formal skill training. Most of them work for the manufacturing, construction

Peasant women harvest their rice paddies in Sanjiang Dong Autonomous County, Guangxi Province.

and service sectors, which mainly require physical labor. Some jobs only last for a certain period, especially those in the construction sector. Then the workers have to find another job. A monitoring report of the National Bureau of Statistics indicated that in 2011 the rural migrant workers who left home to work in cities for the first time had an average age of 26.7 years. In terms of the average term of their current employment, 22.7% mentioned less than one year, 43.1% mentioned one to two years, 43.1% mentioned three to five years, while 13.3% mentioned five years. In addition, due to the urban-rural dual structure, quite a number of rural migrant workers just have the identity as a worker for a certain period and then have to return to home, especially those without good education, the elderly ones that are proficient in farming, and those who have other family members in their hometown. It's worth noting that in recent years migration of rural families is becoming more and more frequent. This is helpful for enhancing the stability of rural migrant workers'employment and living standards. However, for many rural migrant workers who had been doing farm work before they came to cities, they would not like to abandon their farmland, even when they have stable jobs,

Farmers go out for physical work mainly on construction, manufacturing and services.

residences and household registration in urban areas. On the contrary, the rural migrant workers who grew up and have been living in cities and do not know how to do farming would not like to return to their hometowns, even when they do not have a good job in cities. For these people, restriction of household registration and increasingly high housing prices are major obstacles for them to settle down in urban areas.

In China, urbanization has become a major trend. From 1990 to 2000, the urbanization rate had been increasing by one percentage point each year, while, from 2000 to 2010, it had been increasing by 1.36 percentage points each year. This indicates an increasingly accelerating urbanization. In 2011, the population urbanization rate reached 51.27%. It was the first time that urban population exceeded the rural population, while the proportion of employees in the primary industry declined to 38.1%, indicating that the population structure in which rural residents are the dominant proportion would never exist again. In recent years the scale of the floating population has been expanding. For this, the rural migrant workers play a major role. It's predicted that in the coming 30 years, more than 300 million rural population may move to urban areas. However, about 80% of the floating population have rural household registration so that they are referred to as a "passively urbanized population"14. Data from the China Data Center of Tsinghua University released in October 2013 indicated that the household registration urbanization of China was still at a low level, and the population with non-agricultural household registration only accounted for 27.6% of the total population of China, while the ratio of transfer from agricultural registration to non-agricultural household registration only increased by 7.7% during 20 years.

The Chinese government has called for new-model urbanization with a focus on exploration of new ways for in-depth urbanization and solutions of problems concerning the assimilation of the "passively urbanized population" by reforming the household registration system. However, it is not an easy step because in China, the household registration system is still the core of the urban-rural dual system and is attached to an unequal social welfare system. For example, the rural migrant worker and their family members covered by the statistics on urban permanent population enjoy far different employment, education, medical and health care and indemnificatory housing services compared with people with urban household registration. Up to 2012, the coverage rates of the endowment, work-related injury, medical, unemployment and maternity insurance systems for urban employees of rural migrant workers were 14.3%, 24.0%, 16.9%, 8.4% and 6.1% respectively, which were still kept at a low level. Basically, low-rent housing and economically affordable housing are not available to rural migrant workers, nor are the housing accumulation fund system services. To eliminate the disparate treatment due to household registration means to put the floating population under localized management and realize the equalization of public services. Considering the number of floating population and the local bearing capacity and to avoid the appearance of the phenomenon of "slums" that appeared during the urbanization in some countries, this reform should be made in a progressive way. In 2011, the *Circular of the State Council on Promoting*

The new rural community in the seat of Xiaozhi Town, Pingyin County, Shangdong Province in Sept., 2013.

the Reform of Household Registration Management System in a Motivated and Steady Way was put into practice, and related departments, including the National Development and Reform Commission and the Ministry of Human Resources and Social Security, issued related supporting policies. Meanwhile, 18 provinces,autonomous regions and municipalities made specific implementation schemes, and 14 provinces, autonomous regions and municipalities established unified urban and rural household registration systems to open channels for the rural population to finish household registration in urban areas. In accordance with the statistics of the Ministry of Public Security, from 2010 to 2012, a total of 25.05 million (8.35 million each year) rural migrants completed household registration in urban areas. In 2013, the Chinese government clarified the paths to be taken by different cities for urbanization. It promised to fully lift the restrictions of small towns and cities on household registration, lift the restrictions of medium-sized cities, gradually lift the restrictions of metropolises, set reasonable conditions for household registration in megacities, and gradually

Table 2-3-2
Coverage of the Social Security System of Rural Migrant Workers From 2008 to 2012
Unit: %

	2008	2009	2010	2011	2012
Endowment insurance	9.8	7.6	9.5	13.9	14.3
Work-related injury insurance	24.1	21.8	24.1	23.6	24.0
Medical insurance	13.1	12.2	14.3	16.7	16.9
Unemployment insurance	3.7	3.9	4.9	8.0	8.4
Maternity insurance	2.0	2.4	2.9	5.6	6.1

Data source: The *2012 Survey and Monitoring Report on Chinese Rural Migrant Worker*, National Bureau of Statistics.

Table 2-3-3
Age Structure of Rural Migrant Workers From 2008 to 2012
Unit: %

	2008	2009	2010	2011	2012
16-20 years old	10.7	8.5	6.5	6.3	4.9
21-30 years old	35.3	35.8	35.9	32.7	31.9
31-40 years old	24.0	23.6	23.5	22.7	22.5
41-50 years old	18.6	19.9	21.2	24.0	25.6
Above 50 years old	11.4	12.2	12.9	14.3	15.1

Data source: The *2012 Survey and Monitoring Report on Chinese Rural Migrant Worker*, National Bureau of Statistics.

Table 2-3-4
Accommodation Conditions for Rural Migrant Workers From 2008 to 2012
Unit: %

	2008	2009	2010	2011	2012
Dormitory	35.1	33.9	33.8	32.4	32.3
Work shed on construction site	10.0	10.3	10.7	10.2	10.4
Production and operation site	6.8	7.6	7.5	5.9	6.1
Jointly rent house	16.7	17.5	18.0	19.3	19.7
Independently rent house	18.8	17.1	16.0	14.3	13.5
Locally purchased house	0.9	0.8	0.9	0.7	0.6
House in hometown	8.5	9.3	9.6	13.2	13.8
Others	3.2	3.5	3.5	4.0	3.6

Data source: The *2012 Survey and Monitoring Report on Chinese Rural Migrant Worker*, National Bureau of Statistics.

convert rural migrants meeting relevant conditions into urban residents. The last task should be of special importance. Unified measures should be adopted to promote reform of household registration system and equalization of basic public services based on the principles to take a full consideration of local conditions, make progressive efforts, maintain stability, propel increase, and focus on rural migrant population while giving consideration to urban population that work in areas outside the places where their household registrations were made.

Migration of population mainly in form of migration of rural migrant workers is a kind of one-way migration from rural areas to urban areas. It is essentially transfer of rural surplus laborers, which mainly include young and strong males. For example, in 2012, men accounted for 66.4% of the rural migrant workers, while women accounted for 33.6%. By age, as shown in Table 2-3-3, people aged 16 to 20 accounted for 4.9%; those aged 21 to 30 accounted for 31.9%; those aged 31 to 40 accounted for 22.5%; those aged 41 to 50 accounted for 25.6%; those older than 50 accounted for 15.1%. To a large extent, the outflow of young men greatly promoted and accelerated aging and empty-nest tendencies in rural areas, since people left in these areas mainly include the elderly, women and children. A report published by *Farmers' Daily* on March 31, 2012 said that, the number of left-behind children, elderly and women in rural areas respectively reached 50 million, 40 million and 47 million, respectively. The *Report on the Left-behind Children in Rural Areas and Migrant Children in Urban and Rural Areas of China* of the All-China Women's Federation estimated that, based on the data of the 6th national population census made in 2010 there are 61.026 million left-behind children in rural areas, accounting for 37.7% of the rural children and 21.9% of the children of the whole country. Compared with the estimation based on the 1% sampling survey made in 2005, the number of rural left-behind children of the country increased by about 2.42 million during five years, with growth of 4.1%. Among the rural left-behind children, children with one parent going outside to work accounted for 53.3%. Children with both parents going outside to work accounted for 46.7%. Of them, those living with

In Mar., 2014, Sun Liying, the CPPCC member, appealed to the whole society to pay more attention to family education of the children of migrant workers during the two sessions (NPC&CPPCC).

grandparents accounted for 32.7% of the total number of left-behind children; those living with others accounted for 10.7%; those living by themselves accounted for 3.4% (2.057 million). There are a number of problems in urgent need of solutions in rural areas in the urbanization process, such as elderly care, family life of rural migrant workers, development of women, and the raising, education and growth of left-behind children.

Resettled Population under Engineering and Ecological Projects

In addition to the normal population migration types mentioned above, China also has a great number of resettled people due to engineering and ecological projects. The most representative project is the Three Gorges Project, which lasted for 18 years and finally ended in 2010. A total of 1.3976 million people were resettled under the project. Another representative project is the South-to-North Water Diversion Project, which may be the largest cross-basin water diversion project in the world. The land acquisition under the Phase I project concerns a resettlement population of about 440,000 and a production resettlement population of about 570,000. So far, the heaviest task for the resettlement of 345,000 people in the Danjiangkou Reservoir area has been finished. Statistics showed that, since the founding of the New China, more than 86,000 reservoirs have been built up all over the country, including more than 5,000 large- and middle-sized reservoirs and hydropower stations; a total of 23.65 million people enjoyed related follow-up supporting policies. With the addition of the resettled people in the small-sized reservoir areas, there are a total of more than 40 million people resettled from the reservoir areas. Such resettlement has become a major problem concerning people's livelihood and a social problem concerning sustainable development of water conservancy and hydropower programs and social stability in reservoir areas.

The old Yunyang County in Chongqing City was inundated by the rising water after the impoundment of the Three Gorges project in June, 2003.

A square of Gan'en New Community, Xijing Township in Huanghuatan project area of ecological migration and poverty alleviation and development, Gulang County, Gansu Province in Apr, 2013.

Ecological migration is a major way to help residents of areas with harsh ecological conditions to get out of poverty. Meanwhile, it is also an important measure for maintaining sustainable development of ecological environment in areas with lower population-bearing capacity. In 2003, the Chinese government launched the country's first ecological migration project to protect the ecological environment in the Sanjiangyuan (Source of Three Rivers) area, namely the project to return grazing land to grassland in Zhalinghu Town, Madoi County, Qinghai. Up to 2010, the Chinese government has carries out resettlement programs to get more than 7.7 million poverty-stricken people out of poverty. These programs effectively improved the conditions for the living, traffic and electricity use of these people. Since 2008, the resettlement programs have been further promoted. The programs for the resettlement of the people in southern Shaanxi and the Baiyu Mountain area in northern Shaanxi were launched. It is planned that these two programs will last for 10 years with a total investment of more than RMB 100 billion, covering 2.4 million and 392,000 people, almost two times as much as the resettled population under the Three Gorges Project.

Population Flowing to Foreign Countries

In recent years, more and more Chinese people choose to study and live overseas.

Figure 2-3-2 shows, China is now the biggest source of overseas students of many universities in the world. From 1978 to 2011, the total number of Chinese students in foreign universities reached 2.2451 million, accounting for 14% of the total number of global overseas students; about 40% of them returned to China after graduation, while 60% stayed overseas. Since 2008, the number of Chinese students studying overseas has maintained a growth rate of about 20% each year, reaching about 340,000 in 2011 and more than 400,000 in 2012. What's more, more than 90% of such students study overseas at their own expense, and more and more younger students are going abroad.

On the other hand, since the middle and later 1990s, the Chinese laborers have been flowing to the foreign labor service markets all over the world. The *2011 China Trade and External Economic Statistical Yearbook* said that, from 2001 to 2010, a total of 1.9016 million people were sent by national and local companies to work in foreign countries on contracted projects, while 4.4607 million people were covered by overseas labor cooperation programs. Therefore, during this period, a total of 6.3623 million people were engaged in overseas labor.

According to the *Report on Study on Overseas Chinese* of Huaqiao University, during the first 30 years in which the reform and opening-up policies were put into practice, the number of overseas Chinese migrants may reach more than 4.5 million.Currently, there are a total of 45.43 million overseas Chinese all over the world, about 5.3 million in the North American region, including about 3 million migrants who came to the region after 1978. In the first ten years of the 21st century, the number of Chinese in the USA saw a sharp increase by 65.5% over the last ten years, reaching 4.025 million people, ranking fifth among all the ethnic groups in the USA, following white people, black people, Mexicans and Puerto Ricans. The number of immigrants from the Chinese mainland has exceeded the number of Chinese-Americans born in the USA, becoming the biggest Chinese ethnic group in the USA.

A recent report of Pew Research Center (USA) showed that China ranked fourth as a source of immigrants. The report also said that China ranked the second in terms of reception of remittances. The report titled *Changing Patterns of Global Migration and Remittances* analyzed data from the United Nations and the World Bank. It said that as an immigrant-exporting country, China ranked 7th

Figure 2-3-2
Overseas Study in the New Century

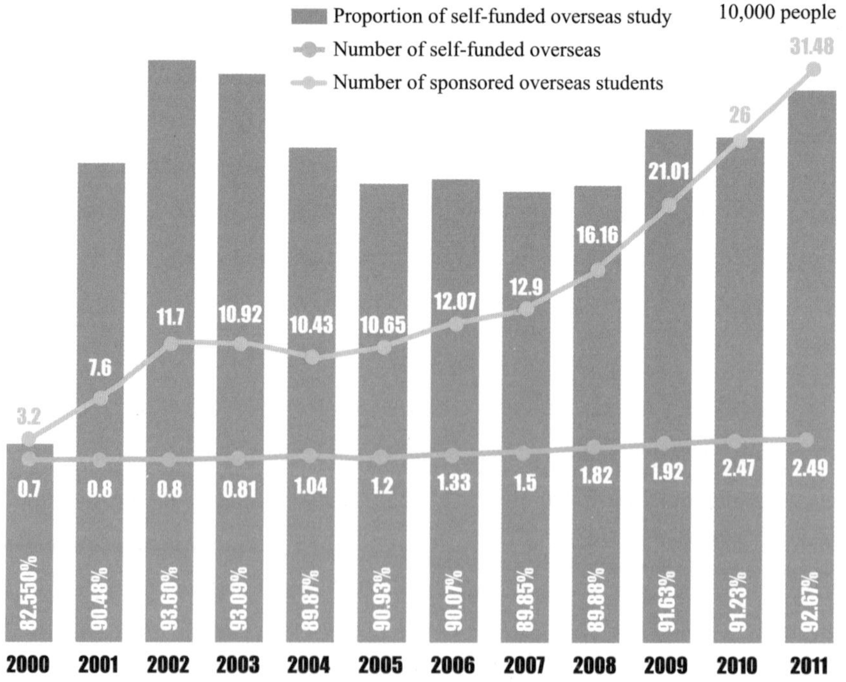

Proportion of self-funded overseas study
Number of self-funded overseas
Number of sponsored overseas students
10,000 people

3.2 7.6 11.7 10.92 10.43 10.65 12.07 12.9 16.16 21.01 26 31.48
0.7 0.8 0.8 0.81 1.04 1.2 1.33 1.5 1.82 1.92 2.47 2.49
82.550% 90.48% 93.60% 93.09% 89.87% 90.93% 90.07% 89.85% 89.88% 91.63% 91.23% 92.67%
2000 2001 2002 2003 2004 2005 2006 2007 2008 2009 2010 2011

Data source: Center for China & Globalization, *Annual Report on the Development of China's Study Abroad (2012)*.

23 years ago, while now 4th, with an increase of emigrants from 4.1 million to 9.2 million, closely following India (14.2 million), Mexico (13.2 million) and Russia (10.8 million). Currently, most people emigrate to wealthy countries, and the USA is still the most popular destination for immigration.15

According to the *Annual Report on Chinese International Migration (2012)* of the Center for China & Globalization, in 2011 the number of the permanent emigrants from China to several countries as main destinations of immigration reached more than 150,000, including 87,017 that have obtained right to permanent residency in the USA, which is the No. 1 destination for Chinese emigration, followed by Canada, Australia and New Zealand. The same year, the number of Chinese business emigrants to other countries exceeded 10,000, while the number of Chinese skilled emigrants to major immigration destinations exceeded 40,000. The report said that since the reform and opening-up policies were put into practice, China has experienced three big waves of emigration. The first wave happened at the beginning of the implementation of the reform and

The Entrepreneurship Week for Chinese Overseas Students in Liaoning Province (Dalian) was inaugurated on Sept 24th, 2008, making a bridge of the employment or self-employment for students abroad.

The Negotiations for Overseas High Technology and High-level Talents was held in Chengdu on Oct. 22nd, 2013. The picture shows that Ma Rupei, the deputy director of Overseas Chinese Affairs Office of the State Council, issued certificates to 20 "Introduced advisers".

opening-up policies, when many people with overseas relatives went abroad. The second wave happened from the end of the 1980s to the end of the 1990s, when many developed countries started to absorb skilled immigrants and business immigrants from China. The third wave happened in the 21st century, featuring large-scale elite emigration, including a great number of business and skilled immigrants as well as students who stayed abroad after graduation. Although the three waves of emigration had different causes, the tendency for continuous talent outflow before China can become a developed country under globalization will not change. Of course, the Chinese government has carried out a number of policies for attracting overseas talent and made remarkable achievements. For example, in 2008, the Chinese government announced to carry out *The Recruitment Program of Global Experts*, which aims to, within five to ten years, attract and support a number of strategic scientists and leading talents that are able to make breakthroughs in key technologies, develop high-tech industries and lead the development of new branches of science to start and operate businesses in various industrial parks for national key innovation programs, key disciplines and key laboratories, central enterprises and state-owned commercial and financial organizations as well as high-tech industrial development zones. In June 2010, the Chinese government released the *National Medium-and Long-Term Program for Talents Development* (2010 to 2020), which aims to enable China to rank among the top countries in attracting overseas talent by 2020. In recent years, the number of returned Chinese students studying abroad each year has been at historical highs. The Organization Department of the CPC Central Committee has taken the lead to carry out the Thousand Talents Program, while the Ministry of Education has carried out the Chang Jiang Scholars Program. Other programs and policies include the Hundred Talents Program led by the Chinese Academy of Sciences, the Program of National Science Fund for Distinguished Young Scholars of the National Natural Science Foundation of China, the Talent Visa policies and the Green Card policies. These programs and policies attract a great deal of overseas talent each year to come to China start and operate businesses. A UN survey found that, when education expenditures account for more than 5% of GNP, research and development expenditures account for more than 1.9% of GNP, research and development fund for each scientist or engineer reaches more than USD 60,000/year, and more than 1,500 people of each million people are scientists engaged in research and development, the amount of overseas talent will increase greatly. It's believed that, through years of efforts, China will certainly meet these conditions.

With rapid development and improvement of its international status, China is attracting more and more foreign people to make investments, start businesses, study and participate in exchange activities in China. The *Annual Report on Chinese International Migration (2012)* showed that up to the end of 2010, there had been 1.02 million foreign people with short-term or long-term stays in China; up to the end of 2011, there had been 4,752 foreign people with Foreigner's Permanent Residence Cards. In 2012, the number of overseas students in China reached about 330,000. It may reach about 880,000 by 2020.

Imbalance in Gender Ratio at Birth

Major Causes for Abnormal Gender Ratio at Birth

High gender ratio at birth has been a major problem in the natural population structure of China since the 1980s. In accordance with the world population structure, a moderately high sex ratio at birth is reasonable. The global gender ratio at birth is 102 to 107 male babies for every 100 female babies, in other words, more boys than girls. However, at higher age groups, death rate of males is higher than that of females. Therefore, at the advanced age groups, there are more females than males. This is an objective law followed by the change of gender ratio of humans. However, too low or too high gender ratio at birth may cause a marriage squeeze, which means some people may be not able to get married throughout their whole lives. The first population census in China in 1953 revealed a gender ratio at birth of 104.9 (meaning 104.9 male babies for every 100 female babies), while the second population census in 1964 showed

Figure 2-4-1
Gender Ratio at Birth Under Six Population Censuses

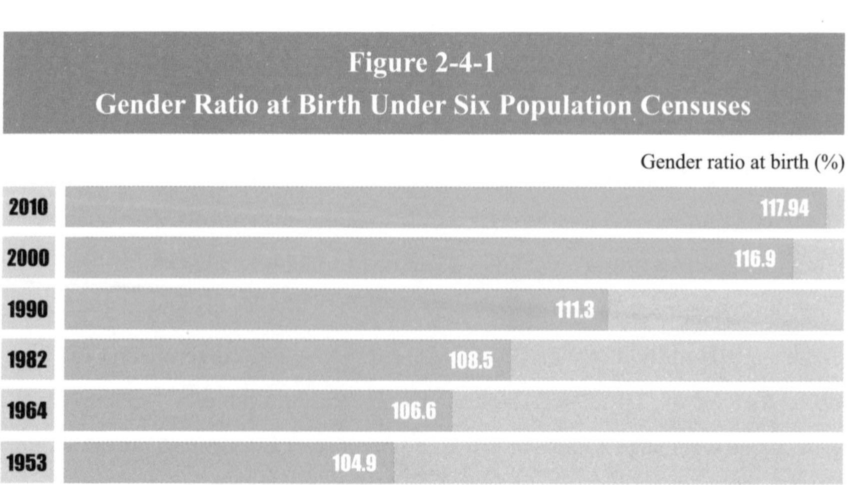

a ratio of 106.6. By 1975, such ratio was 106.54. However, since the 1980s, it has had obvious increases, breaking through 107.11 in 1980 and continuing to increase: 108.5 in 1982; 111.3 in 1990; 116.9 in 2000; 120.56 in 2008, when it peaked, before dropping to 117.94 in 2010. (See Figure 2-4-1)

There may be sufficient reasons to attribute the increasingly higher gender ratio at birth of China since the 1980s to the new population policies issued and implemented during the same period. As the people of many other nations, the Chinese people have the tradition of valuing sons over daughters for carrying on their family lines. However, this traditional concept was not the factor that caused the imbalance in the gender ratio at birth during the first 30 years after the founding of the New China. The strict family planning policies implemented in the 1980s activated the traditional concept that had been buried deeply in the mind of the people, especially the farmers, who wanted more children to get farmland plots that were distributed by family members and expected more sons than daughters in considering that sons might work for their families and take

The traditional view on favoring male heirs is still in many Chinese people's mind.

Laws have been made to protect baby girls.

care of their parents when they grew up. So, many people chose to violate the family planning policy and make prenatal sex selection by abusing B-ultrasonic examination and induced abortion. In some poverty-stricken areas, some newborn babies were also brutally drowned. Therefore, the increase of gender ratio at birth is a result of multiple factors. However, the population policy and the recovery of some family functions are the most important factors.

The Problem of "Bachelors"

The imbalance in gender ratio at birth in the 1980s has been increasingly obvious among the people concerned. The *Social Blue Paper of 2010* released by the Chinese Academy of Social Sciences indicates that, currently, there is a serious imbalance in gender ratio among people under 19, and by 2020, males at marriageable ages will exceed females of the same age by 24 million. At that time, it will be hard for millions of males to find a wife. Meanwhile, the difficulty in finding a wife varies due to the difference in economic strength of

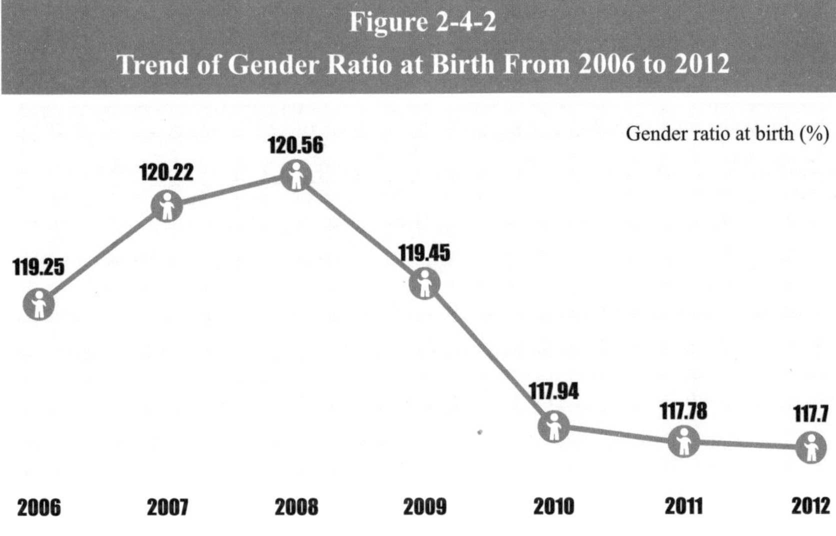

Figure 2-4-2
Trend of Gender Ratio at Birth From 2006 to 2012

different areas. The Institute for Population and Development Studies (IPDS) of the School of Public Policy and Management of Xi'an Jiaotong University made the *Report on Survey on Gender Ratio Imbalance and Social Stability*, which said that, after 2013, the proportion of surplus males will reach more than 10%, meaning that on average 1.2 million males cannot find their first marriage partner each year. In accordance with data on men above the average age for marriage, on average, each administrative village in the western part of China has 10.3 such men, higher than that in the eastern part of China (7.35). By territory, the overall trend of "bachelors" increases from east to west. However, in recent years, as many men in the border areas tend to find a wife in the neighboring countries, the problem has been temporarily relieved, though many such marriages are not based on legitimate procedures. On the other hand, the popularity of online marriage-seeking and outbound tourism makes the phenomenon of "finding a foreign wife" popular in the inland areas of China. At the same time, it drives criminal activities such as trafficking of women and children.

Comprehensive Measures for Imbalance in Gender Ratio at Birth

Long-lasting imbalance of gender ratio at birth will impact social stability. Therefore, it is closely related to the interests of the masses. In recent years, the Chinese government has been paying much attention to the problem and has established the target of normalizing the gender ratio at birth by 2020. For this, a working mechanism featuring accountability of the Party and the government, collaboration of different departments and participation of the masses has been established, while related process evaluation and responsibility assessment for comprehensive management have been enhanced. Meanwhile, activities themed on "care for girls" have been carried out to eliminate sexual discrimination, advocate equality of men and women, extend the concept of fewer and better births, and popularize laws and regulations on protection of the rights of women

A couple at a group wedding made donations to "Spring Buds Project" that helps young girls from poor families to go to school.

and children. Social and economic policies in favor of girls' health and women's development have been made to provide equal opportunities for women in work and social and economic activities. The rural elderly care and pension system should be further improved to reduce the influence of the traditional thinking of "rearing sons to support parents in their old age". Rewards should be provided to families only with one daughter or at most two daughters under the family planning program. Priority should be given to such families under the poverty alleviation, charitable relief, soft loan, employment arrangement and project supporting programs. Social activities for public good, such as the "Happiness Program" and the "Spring Buds Program", should be further promoted. Related measures should be made to encourage husbands to live with their wives' families and protect the rights and interests of women concerning house sites, inheritance of houses and land contracts. Fetal sex diagnosis beyond medical need and termination of pregnancy due to knowledge of gender should be prohibited. Criminal activities such drowning, abandoning and cruelly injuring or killing female babies, abducting and trafficking women and children as well as abusing women giving birth to girls should be strictly punished to protect the legitimate rights and interests of women and children. By taking these comprehensive measures, the gender ratio at birth of China has shown a downward trend since 2009 (See Figure 2-4-2), though there is still a long way to go for a completely normalized gender ratio at birth.

Notes

5. In the Planed Economy period, the Chinese government was forced by pressure in employment to organize the educated youth to leave cities for rural areas. This measure was advocated in the 1950s, widely put into practice in the 1960s, and developed into a political campaign during the "Cultural Revolution" that lasted from 1966 to 1976. Related statistics indicated that, before 1966, there were fewer youth going to the rural areas. However, from 1967 to 1979 (13 years), about 16.5 million young people went to rural areas. (*Revaluation on the Campaign for the Youth Going to Rural Areas*, by Pan Mingxiao, *The Study of Sociology*, Fifth Issue, 2005) . After 1979, most of the educated youth returned to urban areas, while some got married and stayed in rural areas. However, due to the increase of urban poor in the wake of rising layoffs and unemployment, 19.98 million of the 320 million non-agricultural people had still been the urban poor by November, 2002. Therefore the government established the "Three Guarantee Lines" (basic living guarantee for laid-off workers from SOEs and unemployment insurance system and urban resident minimum subsistence allowances) to generally achieve the coverage of all those who qualified.

6. Replacement level is a level at which women would have only enough children to replace themselves. With replacement level fertility, the birth rate will gradually tend to be balanced with the mortality rate. Without international immigration and emigration, the population will stop increasing and keep stable. Such process takes different amounts of time based on the population structure by age. So far, nearly all the developed countries have reached or are even lower than the replacement level, which is usually determined by a total fertility rate of 2.1. For developing countries, which

have high mortality rate, the total fertility rate required for a replacement level is usually higher than 2.1.

7. Fall of marriage rate, and rise of divorce rate, weakened restriction of marriage on sex, lack of attention to the elderly and focus on children, as well as difficulties in family-based elderly care. Change of Urban and Rural Family Structures and Functions of China, Zhejiang Academic Journal, Second Issue, 2005.

8. *Analysis on Change of Contemporary Chinese Family Structure*, by Wang Yuesheng, *Social Science in China*, Fifth Issue, 2007.

9. *Structure of Rural Families and Change of Three-Generation Extended Families*—Based *on Analysis on Data of National Population Census, Southern Population*, First Issue , 2013.

10. The two-member families may also include generation-skipping families, especially those with left-behind elderly and children.

11. The traditional UN standard considered a region to be aging when the population aged above 60 accounted for 10% of its population, while the new standard considers a region to be aging when the population aged above 65 account for 7% of its population. The data on the fifth national population census indicated that, in 2000, China had 88.11 million aged population aged above 65, accounting for 6.96% of the total population, and 130 million population aged above 60, accounting for 10.2% of the total population.

12. In 2000, the average life expectancy of the Chinese people was 71.40 years, five years longer than the world average level and seven years longer than many other developing countries and regions. In 2010, the average life expectancy of the Chinese people was 74.83 years, while that of the world population was 69.6 years, that of high-income countries and regions was 79.8 years and that of middle-income countries and regions was 69.1 years.

13. "Drifters in Beijing" refer to people live and work in Beijing but without household registration in Beijing. Similar phenomenon can be also seen in Shanghai, Guangzhou and other megacities and metropolises.

14. Also called "half-urbanization" or "pseudo-urbanization". In demographic statistics, members of the floating population living in urban areas for more than half a year should be deemed urban population.

15. www.zaobao.com.sg, December 19, 2013. A UN report said that, currently, the number of global migrants has increased from 155 million in 1990 to 214 million in 2010, North American and European countries are still the main destinations, while Mexico, India, Russia, China and Bangladesh are the biggest immigrant-exporting countries. Please refer to the report made by UN Secretary-General Ban Ki-moon at the 46th conference of the Commission on Population and Development of UN themed on "Trends in Migration: Demographic Aspects" held on April 22, 2013.

Polarization and Transformation of Social Structure

Polarization and transformation have become the primary features of social change in China since the reform and opening-up policies were put into practice. With market-oriented reforms and the adjustment of ownership structures and the enhancement of social mobility, both the connotation and denotation of the working class have changed, while the number of farmers has dropped steadily and many new social classes have appeared. Therefore, the so-called "Two Classes and One Stratum" during the planned economy period is long gone. Accordingly, in addition to traditional mass organizations and social organizations, many new economic organizations and social organizations have emerged, and grassroots self-governing organizations have enjoyed prosperous development. The traditional social organization pattern is being replaced by a new one. With continuous industrialization, marketization and rapid adjustment of economic and industrial structures, the employment structure and mode have been greatly changed. Meanwhile the diversification of allocation has caused an obvious gap between the rich and the poor throughout society. Along with this is unbalanced rural and urban development and regional development, with growing problems concerning relative poverty.

Employment Structure, Urbanization Rate and Industrial Structure

Retardation of Urbanization During the Planned Economy Period and Related Reasons

International experience shows that employment structure, and urban and rural population structure change along with industrial structure. Industrial structure influences employment structure as well as urban and rural population structure. However, for a long time, the changes of these structures in China deviated from this international rule: there was little change in the employment structure and the urban and rural population structure along with the fast change of the industrial structure. China adopted the planned economy system before it began reforms. At that time, it carried out the catching-up-oriented industrialization strategy led by the development of heavy industries, which enabled the country to establish an independent and integrated national economic system and industrial system in a short time. This can be proved by the structure of the primary, secondary and tertiary industries, which was 50.5:20.9:28.6 in 1952 and 30.1:48.5:21.4 in 1980, respectively. Over about 30 years, the proportion of the primary industry dropped by 20.4 percentage points, while that of the secondary industry increased by 27.6 percentage points and that of the tertiary industry dropped by 7.2 percentage points. This was an extremely unbalanced growth model, which allowed secondary industry to play a dominant role. In the same period, the employment structure of tertiary industry changed from 83.5:7.4:9.1 to 68.7:18.2:13.1, with the proportion of urban population increased from 12.46% to 19.39%. Because of low flexibility of employment in heavy industry, the employment proportions of secondary industry didn't have

Table 3-1-1
The Industrial Structure, Employment Structure and Urbanization of China

Year	Industrial Output Value Structure			Industrial Employment Structure			Urban Employment Proportion	Percentage of Urban Population
	I	II	III	I	II	III		
1952	50.5	20.9	28.6	83.5	7.4	9.1	12.0	12.46
1955	46.3	22.4	29.3	83.3	8.6	8.1	12.5	13.48
1960	23.4	44.5	32.1	66.0	15.9	18.1	23.6	19.75
1965	37.9	35.1	27.0	81.6	8.4	10.0	17.9	17.98
1970	35.2	40.5	24.3	80.8	10.2	9.0	18.3	17.38
1975	32.4	45.7	21.9	77.2	13.5	9.3	21.5	17.34
1980	30.1	48.5	21.4	68.7	18.2	13.1	23.7	19.39
1985	28.4	42.9	28.7	62.4	20.8	16.8	25.7	23.71
1990	27.1	41.3	31.5	60.1	21.4	18.5	26.3	26.41
1995	20.0	47.2	32.9	52.2	23.0	24.8	28.0	29.04
2000	15.0	45.9	39.0	50.0	22.5	27.5	32.1	36.22
2005	12.1	47.4	40.5	44.8	23.8	31.4	36.0	42.99
2010	10.1	46.7	43.2	36.7	28.7	34.6	45.6	49.95

expected growth nor rapid growth of proportions of output value. In primary industry, it was hard for surplus laborers in rural areas to be transferred to other places, which is increasingly becoming a more serious problem with the increase of population. This is the biggest difference from the industrialization-oriented economy led by light industry. Affected by this, urbanization has an especially slow progress. Cities are main locations of tertiary industry, especially the service sector. For about 30 years, at the same time of continuous industrialization, the

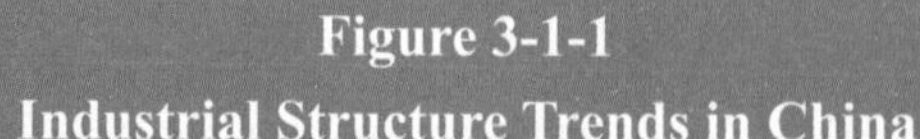

Figure 3-1-1
Industrial Structure Trends in China

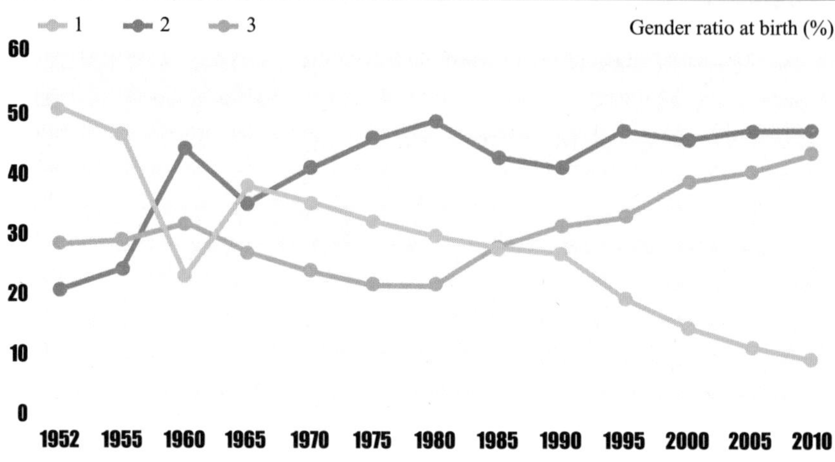

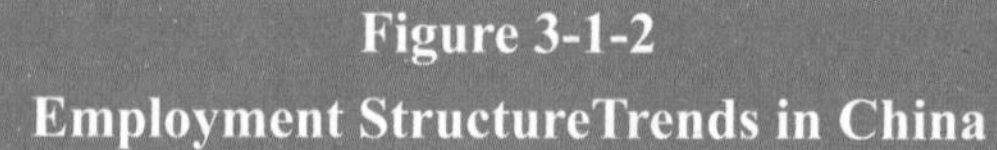

Figure 3-1-2
Employment StructureTrends in China

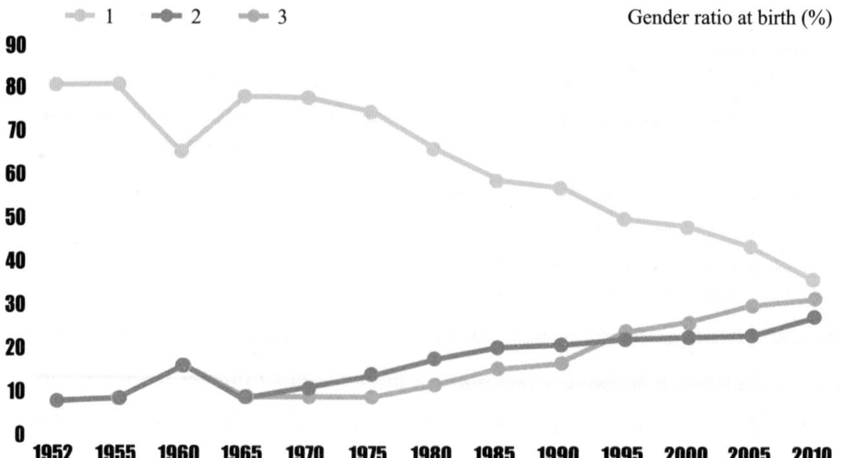

Figure 3-1-3
Urban and Rural Population Distribution in China

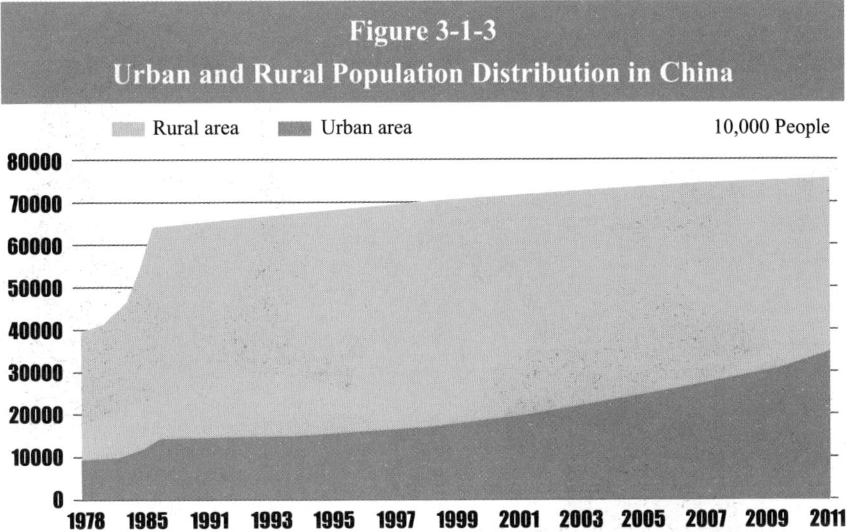

Table 3-1-2
Comparison with Other Countries in Terms of Industrialization and Urbanization

	Proportion of Industrial Output to GDP		Percentage of Urban Population		Per Capita GDP (US$)
	1965	1995	1965	1995	1995
Low-income countries	28	38	17	29	430
Middle-income countries	34	35	42	60	2390
High-income countries	42	32	71	75	24930
World's average	40	33	36	45	4880
China	39	48	18	30	620
India	22	29	19	27	340
Thailand	23	40	33	20	2740

Data source:
World Bank,1991,*World Development Report 1991*,New York:Oxford Universtiy Press.
World Bank,1997,*World Development Report 1997*,New York:Oxford Universtiy Press.

The Decision by the Third Plenary Session of the 18th Central Committee of the Communist Party of China proposed that market must play a decisive role in resource allocation.

proportion of output value of the tertiary industry declined instead of increasing. This shows that, to some extent, the traditional industrialization strategy of China is a kind of counter-urbanization. Meanwhile, the employment proportion of the tertiary industry showed a slight increase during the same period. This should be a result of low-end and labor-intensive development in this field, reflecting a labor surplus in urban areas. Otherwise, it is impossible to explain why China has a far lower urbanization level than that of other economies under the seemingly same industrialization level.16

Coordination and Promotion since the Reform and Opening-up

Since reform and opening-up and the implementation of the market economic system in China, the market has been playing a fundamental role in resource allocation. In November 2013, it was proposed at the Third Plenary Session of the 18th Central Committee of the CPC that the market should play a decisive role in resource allocation. This is a major theoretical breakthrough of the CPC. It is believed that it will have profound influence on the all-around and in-depth reform of China.

Through a rectification process, China's employment structure and industrial structure are being coordinated, while population urbanization is accelerating. This is reflected thusly:

—The proportion of output value of the primary industry saw a decline, from 30.1% in 1980 to 27.1%, 15.1% and 10.1% in 1990, 2000 and 2010, with an annual average drop of 0.67 percentage point; the

Great efforts were made to readjust agricultural industry structure and develop the three-dimensional agritourism in Matan District, Luzhou City, Sichuan Province in March, 2014.

The research center of Chinese Academy of Science predicted that China's GDP would grow at an annual rate of 7.6% in 2014.

proportion of employment of the industry saw a decline, too, from 68.7% to 60.1%, 50.0% and 36.7%, with an annual average drop of 1.07 percentage points. The decline of the proportion of employment was faster than that of output value, indicating that the rural surplus laborers are migrating to non-agricultural industries at a fast speed. As mentioned earlier, the tendency for by-business of rural households during this period should not be ignored.

—The proportion of output value of the tertiary industry saw a fast increase, from 21.4% in 1980 to 31.5%, 39.0% and 43.2% in 1990, 2000 and 2010, more than doubling during 30 years, with an annual average growth of 0.73 percentage point; the proportion of employment of the industry saw an increase, too, from 13.1% to 18.5%, 27.5% and 34.6%, with an annual average growth of 0.72 percentage point. This indicates that the industrial structure and employment structure of China are being normalized. It also shows the acceleration and expansion of urbanization. During the same period, the proportion of urban employment increased year by year from 23.7% in 1980 to 26.3%, 32.1% and 45.6% in 1990,

2000 and 2010, respectively, while the proportion of urban population increased from 19.39% to 29.04%, 36.22% and 49.95%, respectively with an annual average growth of 0.73 and 1.02 percentage points. Since the 1990s, the increase of the urban population has been faster than the increase of urban employment, indicating that the household registration system is gradually losing its rigidity, and more rural families are migrating to urban areas.

—At the same time, the proportion of output value of secondary industry was trending towards stability, with slight decline, from 48.5% in 1980 to 46.7% in 2010; the proportion of employment saw an increase, from 18.2% to 28.7%, with an annual average growth of 3.5 percentage points. This indicates that, along with the market-oriented reform and the integration of China into the global economy, the internal structure of the secondary industry of China had deeply changed so that manufacturing developed quickly and its labor resource advantage had been given full play. With increasing foreign investment and enhanced global economic integration, China has become a "factory of the world". According to IHS Global Insight, an American economic consulting company, in 2010, the output of China's manufacturing sector accounted for 19.8% of the output of the global manufacturing sector, taking the place of the USA to become the leading country in the global manufacturing sector. However, China's manufacturing sector focuses on the middle- and low-end products based on labor-intensive production. At the same time, with fast increase of investment in fixed assets, China's construction sector shows a tendency for a prosperous development. The two sectors mentioned above, which enjoy flexible employment and labor-intensive production, have contributed to the increase of the employment proportion of the secondary industry in these years.

Figure 3-1-4
Proportions of Output Value and Employment of the Primary Industry

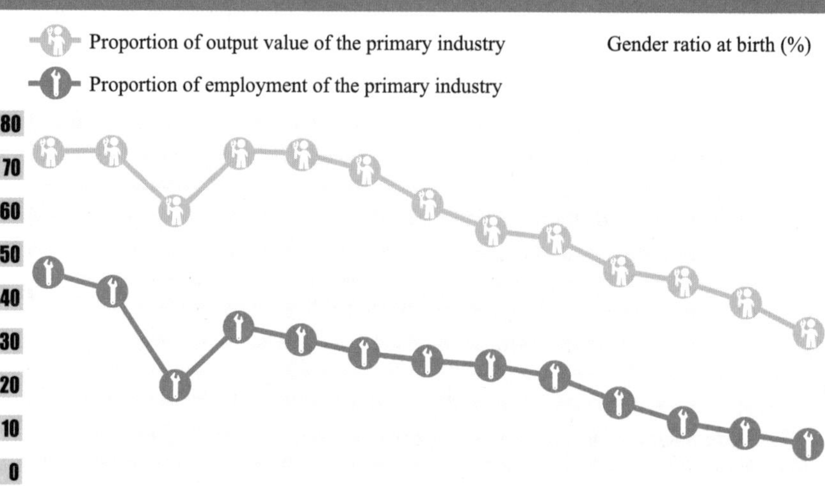

Figure 3-1-5
Proportion of Urban Employment, Urbanization Rate and Proportions of Employment of the Secondary and Tertiary Industries of China

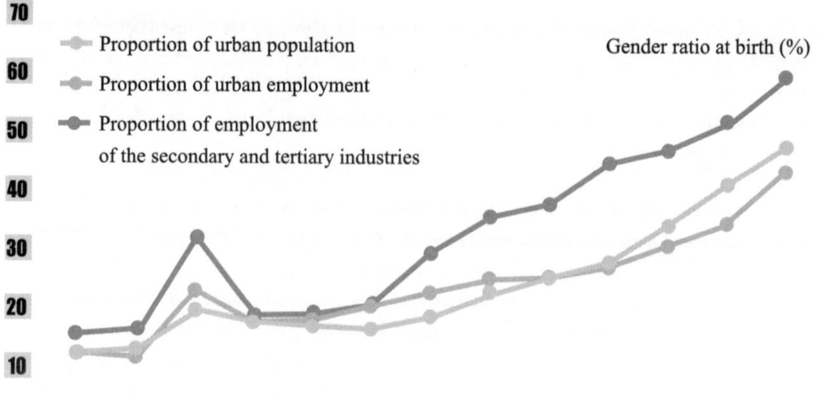

Occupational Structure and Social Stratification

Occupational Classification and Structure

Under the economic environment featuring an open market, the employment structure is continuously being adjusted alongside the changes of the industrial structure. Meanwhile, scientific and technological progress, industrial upgrading and mutual promotion between marketization and socialization leads to an increasingly specific social division of labor and frequent changes in occupational structure. This is highlighted in China after the reform and opening-up policies were put into practice. Before the 1980s, the planned economy

The National Joint Session of Ministers of Propaganda from Vocational Colleges was held in Neusoft Institute of Information Technology, Nanhai (now renamed as Guangdong Neusoft Institute) in Foshan City, Guangzhou Province on Nov, 21st in 2013.

lasted for more than 30 years, during which there was only one occupational classification standard, namely the *Technical Grade Standards for Workers*. From 1982, when the new *Occupational Classification Standards* were issued, to 2005, China had amended the occupational classification system or made related laws and regulations ten times.

Occupational classification can be made by sector, or by industry. In the period when there were only a few of types of occupations, occupation was synonymous to industry. Today occupation and industry are two concepts that have similarities and differences. Occupations can be classified by industry. The *General Standards of the People's Republic of China on Occupational Classification* (hereinafter referred to as the Standards), issued in 1999, made a breakthrough by adopting new principles instead of the traditional mode for occupational classification. Before that, occupational classification was made mainly by industrial regulatory authorities, competent administration departments and units as well as employment forms. The new principle uses identity of job nature as a standard for occupational classification. It was the first time that scientific division and classification of occupations of the whole society were made to fully reflect the social occupational structure of China since reform and opening-up. The Standards classify the occupations of China into eight categories, including 1,838 subclasses under 413 classes of 66 subcategories. In details:

Category I. Leaders of state organs, Party-mass organizations, enterprises and public institutions, including five subcategories, 16 classes and 25 subclasses;

Category II. Professional technical personnel, including 14 subcategories, 115 classes and 379 subclasses;

Category III. Office clerks and related personnel, including four subcategories, 12 classes and 45 subclasses;

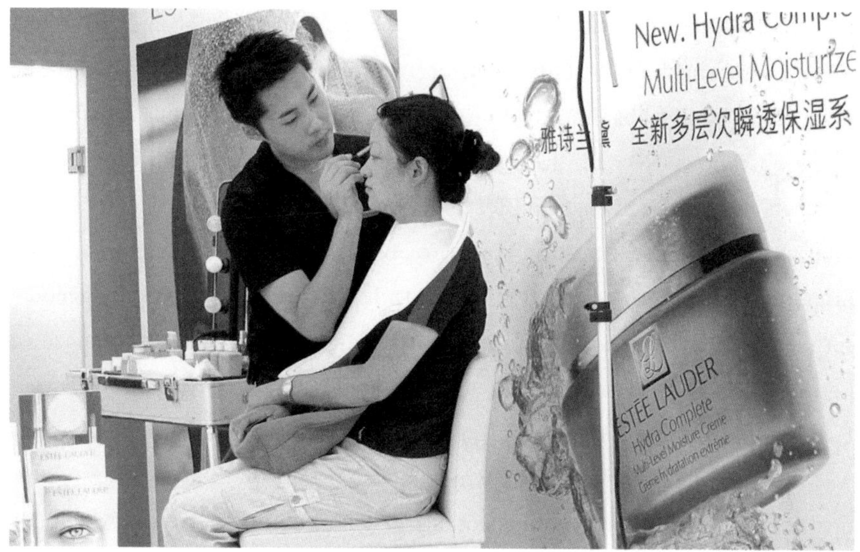

"Image designer" has officially become a new profession in China.

Category IV. Business and service staff, including eight subcategories, 43 classes and 147 subclasses;

Category V. Production personnel in agricultural, forestry, animal husbandry and fishery and water conservancy sectors, including six subcategories, 30 classes and 121 subclasses;

Category VI. Operators of production and transportation equipment and related personnel, including 27 subcategories, 195 classes and 1,119 subclasses;

Category VII. Military servicemen, including one subcategory, one class and one subclass;

Category VIII. Other employees, including one subcategory, one class and one subclass.

In terms of occupational structure, the occupational classification has three characteristics. First, the technical and skill-based occupations play an important role. The category of "operators of production and transportation equipment and related personnel" covers 60.88% of occupations, which are distributed in the main fields of industrial production and mainly deal with technical and skill-based operations. Second, the tertiary industry includes a small proportion of occupations, which only account for about 8% of all occupations. The secondary industry includes the largest proportion of occupations. Third, there are a small proportion of knowledge-based and high-tech occupations, which only account for at most 3% of all occupations. Actually, the appearance and increase of knowledge-based and high-tech occupations are obvious in emerging industries. For example, there is a class between the traditional white-collar and blue-collar workers, known as the grey-collar workers, who mainly work in the information, design and automotive engineering sectors, including electronic engineers, software development engineers, decoration designers, e-commerce operators, multimedia workers, computer network technology personnel, web designers and developers, digital imaging technicians, industrial product designers, jewelry designers and senior car maintenance technicians. These occupations are all leading emerging occupations. Statistics in April 2007 showed that China had 1,989 occupations. Now there should be more than 2,000 occupations in China. Generally, the occupational change in the new period of China has two obvious new characteristics: fast upgrading and increasing subdivision. Some occupations in traditional industries have seen a decrease, while some occupations have silently disappeared. The definitions of some occupations have changed. For example, "nanny" has been changed into "household service personnel", and "barber" has been changed into "hair stylist". Some occupations have been further divided. For example, management of enterprises include chairman, general manager, CEO, department manager and project manager. Some new occupations have been derived from emerging industries. Along with social development, the tertiary industry focusing on services is leading to the appearance of more new occupations.

Social Stratification Based on Accupational Structure

In modern society, occupational structure serves as a fundamental factor for social stratification. The change of occupational structure mentioned above indicates that since the reform and opening-up of China, the biggest change of social stratification should be the shifting between the classes of farmers and industrial workers, which should be a result of industrialization under a relatively balanced industrial structure.

As indicated by Table 3-2-1, Figure 3-2-1 and Figure 3-2-2, from 1982 to 2010, the proportion of people engaged in the agriculture, forestry, animal husbandry, fishery and water conservancy sectors under the seven occupational groups of Category V saw a decline from 71.98% to 48.13%, with a drop of 23.85 percentage points; the proportion of operators of production and transportation equipment and related personnel under Category VI saw an increase from 15.99% to 22.49%, with a growth of 6.5 percentage points.

A job fair for farmers and unemployed people in Xuzhou City, Jiangsu Province. The scene was filled with people.

Figure 3-2-3 indicates that, the decline of the proportion of the personnel under Category V experienced an increasingly accelerated process: the decline had been accelerating year by year since the 1990s. The proportion of personnel under Category VI showed a big fluctuation by first declining and then increasing; the increasing trend appeared at the beginning of the 21st century. It is mainly because the reform of the economic system in the new period began in rural areas that the change of industrial structure and employment structure in rural areas was earlier than that in urban areas. In addition, the reform of state-owned enterprises in the 1990s resulted in a great number of laid-off workers. Therefore, it was not until the completion of the program for re-employment of laid-off workers and the end of the difficult time of the reform of the economic system that the proportion of the personnel under Category VI increased. In 2010, the proportion had a growth of 6.66 percentage points compared with that ten years before. However, it is obvious that the speed of the increase of the proportion

Taiwanese started large shoe factories in Guigang City, Guangxi Province due to its cheap labor.

of the personnel under Category VI is slower than the speed of decline of the proportion of the personnel under Category V. This is because during this period, the tertiary industry experienced fast development, and quite a number of laid-off workers under Category V and VI were transferred to Category IV, while the proportions of personnel under Category II and III saw some increase and the proportions of personnel under Category I and VII saw little change. The changes indicate that, in the last more than 10 years, China's urbanization has made great progress while industrialization has entered a new stage. However, as mentioned above, the personnel under Category V still accounted for nearly 50%, and more than 90% of them were production personnel of the planting industry, indicating a low-level agricultural modernization and the need for long-term hard work for urbanization. Meanwhile, the by-business of rural laborers and the changes in their age and gender structures during this period are also noteworthy.

Concerning urbanization, as mentioned above, the household registration shows that quite a number of industrial workers and people working in the business and service sectors are rural migrant workers with rural household registration (most of them are young males). This is the biggest difference between before and after reform. Before reform, almost all the urban workers were urban residents (with non-agricultural registration). After reform, the structure of the farmers' group changed. "Along with the appearance of rural enterprises, rural workers (farmer workers) who stayed in rural areas and did not farm appeared. After 1992, a great number of farmers flooded into cities. They were rural migrant workers who did not farm and left their hometowns. Statistics indicate that, in 2008, China had a total of 225 million rural migrant workers, including 85 million (37.7%) working in local enterprises and 140 million (62.3%) working in cities. Rural migrant workers account for a large percentage of a total of more than 400 million blue-collar workers in the secondary and tertiary industries. In the construction, mining, environmental sanitation, textile, clothes manufacturing, toy manufacturing and catering service sectors, rural migrant workers are in the majority, or the overwhelming majority."17

Rural migrant workers form a special social stratum among industrial workers and the employees of the business and service sectors. They are workers with rural household registration, and a majority of them are given less pay and welfare than that provided to local employees with non-agricultural household registration in the same workplace. The effect of such difference is magnified in the labor-intensive sectors and the business and service sectors, where rural migrant workers become low-cost laborers with unlimited sources. That's why China became the so called "factory of the world".

Another obvious change of China's social stratification since reform and opening-up is the emerging of many new social classes, including people who start private science and technology businesses and related technical personnel, managerial and technical staff of foreign-funded enterprises, the self-employed, private entrepreneurs, employees of intermediary organizations and freelance professionals. Many members of the new social classes are from the classes of workers, farmers, cadres and intellectuals. They are mainly engaged in businesses under non-public ownership, with high income but unstable career and status. It is estimated that at the beginning of the 21 century, the new social classes include a total of about 50 million people, who, together with 100 million people engaged in related industries, control or manage capital of about RMB 10 trillion, account for more than 50% of technical patents of the country, directly and indirectly contribute 1/3 of the national tax revenue, and provide job opportunities for more than 50% of the new employees every year. They have become a major force for China's economic and social development, and the force is continuing to expand.

Table 3-2-1 Change of Structure of Major Occupational Groups of China From 1982 to 2010
Unit: %

Occupation	1982	1990	2000	2010
1. Leaders of state organs, Party-mass-organizations, enterprises and public institutions	1.56	1.75	1.67	1.77
2. Professional technical personnel	5.07	5.31	5.70	6.84
3. Office clerks and related personnel	1.30	1.74	3.10	4.32
4. Business and service staff	4.01	5.41	9.18	16.17
5. Production personnel in agricultural, forestry, animal husbandry and fishery and water conservancy sectors	71.98	70.58	64.46	48.13
6. Operators of production and transportation equipment and related personnel	15.99	15.16	15.83	22.49
7. Other employees	0.09	0.04	0.07	0.10
Total	100	100	100	100

Figure 3-2-1
Structure of Major Occupational Groups of China in 1982

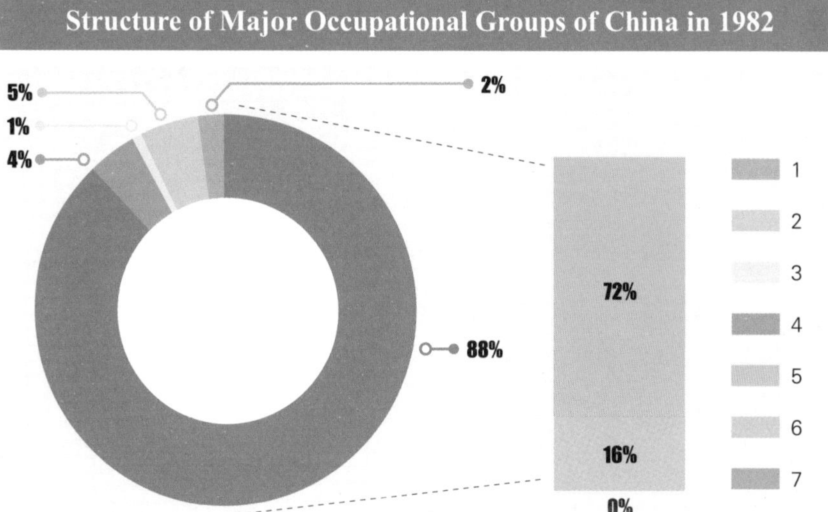

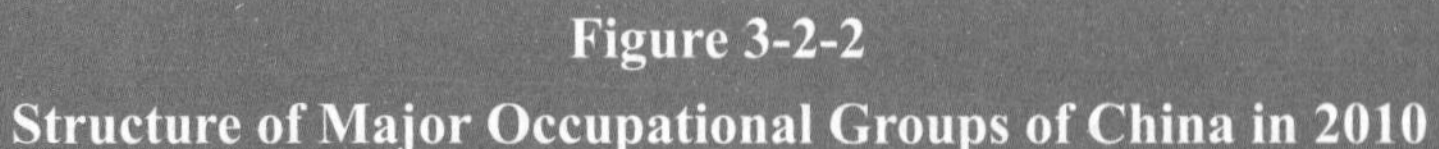

Figure 3-2-2
Structure of Major Occupational Groups of China in 2010

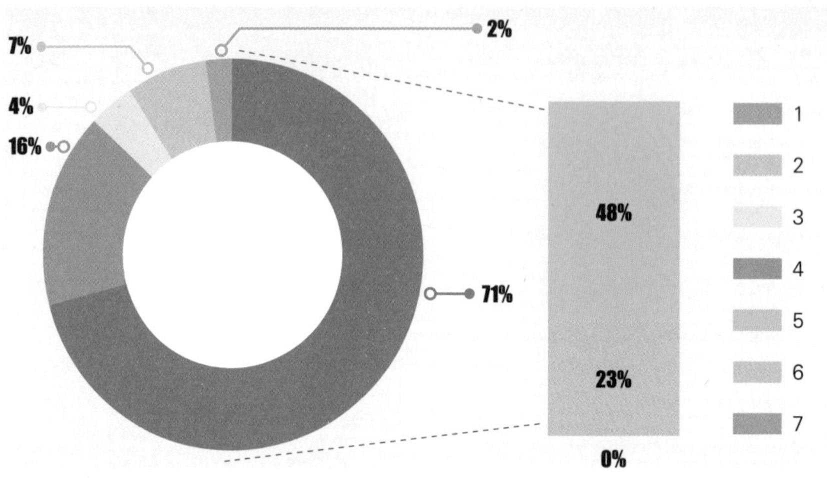

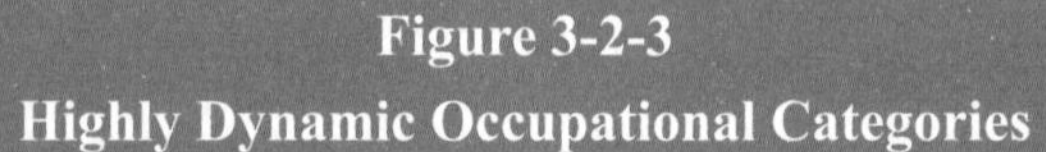

Figure 3-2-3
Highly Dynamic Occupational Categories

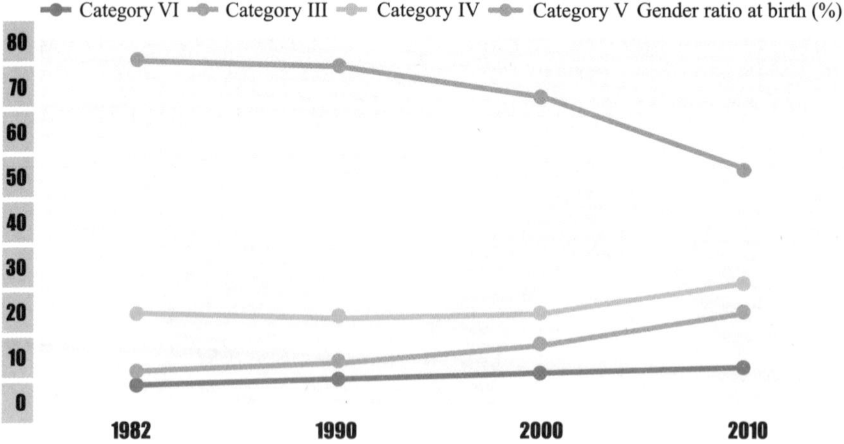

The middle class

The rising of new social classes promotes the expansion of the middle class mainly consisting of management personnel and intellectuals (ie, white-collar workers). This class has different names in China and abroad. The late sociologist Lu Xueyi said the middle class of China includes middle- and high-ranking staff (such as professional technical personnel and civil servants), most of the private entrepreneurs and part of the individual business operators, with an annual increase of about eight million people, and annual growth of proportion in social stratification of about one percentage point. Currently, this social class accounts for about 22% of society, and this proportion may reach 35%to 40% by 2020. A total of about six to seven million graduates of institutions of higher learning every year add to the middle class. Another sociologist Li Qiang said the middle class of China only accounts for less than 15% of the total employed

Today, white-collar class has been the majority of the fast-growing middle class in China.

population; it mainly includes the traditional cadre and intellectual classes (including professional technical personnel), the "new middle class", state-owned enterprises with good operation performance, joint-equity enterprises, other enterprises, companies and units with good operation performance, and individual and private business operators. Figure 3-2-1 and Figure 3-2-2 directly show the expansion of the middle class. From 1982 to 2010, the proportion of the Category V and VI groups saw a decline from about 88% to about 71%, while the proportion of Category I, II, III and IV groups saw an increase from about 12% to about 29%, the change of the proportion of the Category VII group can be ignored.

Generally, whether the pyramid-shaped structure (Figure 3-2-4) proposed by people like Lu Xueyi or the reversed-T-shaped structure (Figure 3-2-5) proposed by people like Li Qiang, a consensus has been reached that the social stratification still features an oversized foundation and an undersized middle class, which is far from the ideal structure that features small proportions of

Figure 3-2-4
Pyramid-shaped Structure Proposed by Lu Xueyi

Figure 3-2-5
Reversed-T-shaped Structure Proposed by Li Qiang

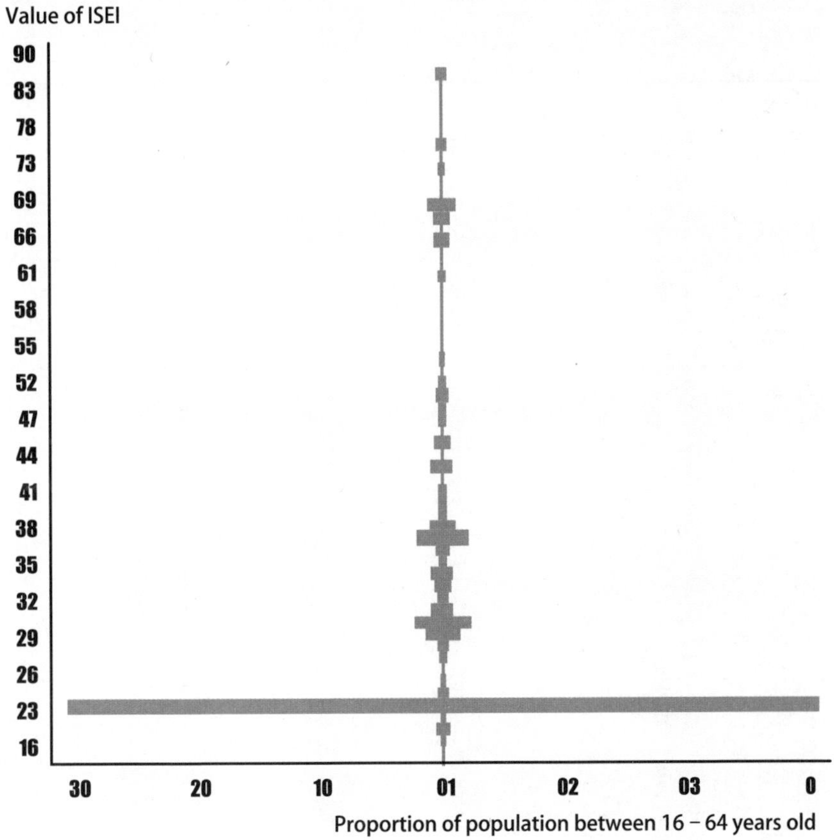

top and foundational classes and a large proportion of middle class. Despite a tendency for a shrinking foundational class and expanding middle class, the household registration system results in different social stratification systems in urban and rural areas. The middle class mainly resides in cities, while rural migrant workers are in an awkward status with an unclear identity. It seems that it will take a long time to build a brand-new modern social stratification structure in China. However, similar to the pyramid-shaped structure, in the reversed-T-shaped structure, 64.7% of people were at a low ISEI level, obviously

Table 3-2-2

Proportion of Employees with Different Education Background in Different Sectors in 2010

	The Illiterate	Primary School	Junior High School	Senior High School	Junior College	Undergraduate	Postgraduate
Total	**1.00**	**1.00**	**1.00**	**1.00**	**1.00**	**1.00**	**1.00**
Agriculture, forestry, animal husbandry and fishery	0.89	0.75	0.50	0.20	0.04	0.01	0.01
Mining	0.00	0.01	0.01	0.02	0.02	0.01	0.01
Manufacturing	0.04	0.09	0.19	0.24	0.18	0.14	0.13
Electricity, gas and water production and supply	0.00	0.00	0.00	0.02	0.03	0.02	0.01
Construction	0.02	0.05	0.07	0.05	0.04	0.03	0.02
Transportation, warehousing and postal service	0.01	0.01	0.04	0.06	0.04	0.03	0.02
Information transmission, computer service and software	0.00	0.00	0.00	0.01	0.03	0.04	0.05

Wholesale and retail sales	0.02	0.04		0.17	0.14	0.09	0.05
Hotel and catering services	0.01	0.01		0.04	0.02	0.01	0.00
Financial business	0.00	0.00		0.01	0.04	0.06	0.06
Real estate	0.00	0.00		0.01	0.02	0.02	0.01
Leasing and business services	0.00	0.00		0.01	0.02	0.03	0.04
Scientific research, technical service and geological prospecting	0.00	0.00		0.00	0.01	0.03	0.07
Water conservancy, environment and public facility management	0.00	0.00		0.01	0.01	0.01	0.01
Resident services and other services	0.01	0.01		0.03	0.01	0.01	0.00
Education	0.00	0.00		0.03	0.13	0.21	0.28
Health, social security and social welfare	0.00	0.00		0.02	0.07	0.06	0.07
Culture, sports and entertainment	0.00	0.00		0.01	0.01	0.02	0.02
Public management and social organization	0.00	0.00		0.04	0.14	0.17	0.13
International organization	0.00	0.00		0.00	0.00	0.00	0.00

In May, 2014, Ministry of Education of the People's Republic of China initialed the transformation of colleges and universities that more than a half of the 1200 national colleges and universities would transfer their focus into vocational education to develop skilled talents.

distinguished from the other groups. Most of these people are farmers with large areas of farmland. Urbanization and education development are the biggest boosters for the expansion of the middle class. As shown in Table 3-2-2, the agriculture, forestry, animal husbandry and fishery sectors employed more than 70% of the illiterate and half-illiterate population of the country. The more opportunities for people to get access to education, the more chances for them to get a job in the education sector, public management, social organizations and the manufacturing sectors. In accordance with the Institute of Labor Science of the Ministry of Human Resources and Social Security of the People's Republic of China, currently, of all the occupational groups, professional technical personnel receive the longest education, at about 13.4 years, followed by the office clerks and related personnel, who averagely receive about 12.5 years of education. The production personnel in agricultural, forestry, animal husbandry and fishery and water conservancy sectors receive the shortest education, which averages 7.7 years, not enough for finishing junior high school study.

Income Distribution and Social Polarization

Income Distribution Structure and Change of Income Composition

The current social stratification of China is fully proved by the structure of residents' income distribution. For example, the ranking of the average salary for employees of urban units in different sectors in 2010 (Table 3-3-1) shows that, based on the costs of human resources in different occupations, the work ability and the status of sector, the 19 sectors ranked by average salary for employees were as follows (from high to low): finance; information transmission, computer

Salary conditions in China in 2013: The salary of financial industry was ten times more than the average salary.

services and software; scientific research, technical services and geological prospecting; electricity, gas and water production and supply; mining; culture, sports and entertainment; transportation, warehousing and postal service; health, social security and social welfare; leasing and business services, education, public administration and social organizations, the real estate industry, wholesale and retail, manufacturing, residential and other services; construction; water conservancy, environment and public facility management; hotel and catering services; agriculture, forestry, animal husbandry and fishery. The sectors with lower admission threshold, fiercer market competition and less requirements for skills provide lower salaries for workers; on the contrary, the sectors with higher monopoly, higher admission threshold and more requirements for skills provide higher salary for workers. The average salary of the financial sector is 1.92 times as much as the national average salary (RMB 36,539), and 4.2 times as much as the average salary provided by the agriculture, forestry, animal husbandry and fishery sectors. The average salary of the information transmission, computer services and software sectors is 1.76 times more than the national average, and 3.85 times as much as that provided by the agriculture, forestry, animal husbandry and fishery sectors. Results of an investigation program carried out by the National Bureau of Statistics of the People's Republic of China in the beginning of the 21st century indicated that, among the high-income population in cities, leaders of enterprises and public institutions accounted for 31.0%; professional technical personnel accounted for 25.2%; the free-lance professionals accounted for 17.8%; office clerks and related personnel accounted for 9.5%; business service personnel accounted for 8.5%; production and transportation equipment operators accounted for 4.4%; other types of personnel accounted for 3.5%; and production personnel of agriculture, forestry, animal husbandry, fishery and water conservancy sector accounted for 0.1%. The data indicate that the current occupational structure and social stratification (including economic status of social classes) of China highly coincide with each other. In addition, the system of ownership of the means of production also has influence on the difference in salary. Generally, private businesses provide low salaries for their employees. In 2012, the average salaries of private businesses only accounted for 61.5% of that of non-private businesses.

Table 3-3-1
Ranking of the Average Salaries for Employees of Urban Units in Different Sectors in 2010

Sector	Average Salary (RMB)
Financial business	70,146
Information transmission, computer service and software	64,436
Scientific research, technical service and geological prospecting	56,376
Electricity, gas and water production and supply	47,309
Mining	44,196
Culture, sports and entertainment	41,428
Transportation, warehousing and postal service	40,466
Health, social security and social welfare	40,232
Leasing and business services	39,566
Education	38,968
Public management and social organization	38,242
Real estate	35,870
Wholesale and retail sales	33,635
Manufacturing	30,916
Resident services and other services	28,206
Construction	27,529
Water conservancy, environment and public facility management	25,544
Hotel and catering services	23,382
Agriculture, forestry, animal husbandry and fishery	16,717

Table 3-3-2 Change of Composition of Urban Resident's Income of China Unit: %					
Indicator	**1990**	**1995**	**2000**	**2010**	**2011**
Total income	100.0	100.0	100.0	100.0	100.0
Salary income	75.8	79.2	71.2	65.2	64.3
Net operating income	1.5	1.7	3.9	8.1	9.2
Income from property	1.0	2.1	2.0	2.5	2.7
Transfer income	21.7	17.0	22.9	24.2	23.8

Table 3-3-3 Change of Composition of Rural Resident Income in China Unit: %					
Indicator	**1990**	**1995**	**2000**	**2010**	**2011**
Total income	100.0	100.0	100.0	100.0	100.0
Salary income	14.0	15.1	22.3	29.9	30.2
Household business operating income	82.4	80.3	71.6	60.8	60.4
Income from property	3.6	1.8	1.4	2.5	2.3
Transfer income		2.8	4.7	6.8	7.1

In China, the difference in salaries is not enough to explain the difference in urban and rural resident income, because the resident's income also includes other forms of non-salary incomes, including the operating income, income from property and transfer income. Generally, in the urban resident's income, the salary income takes a smaller percent; it was 64.3% in 2011, 11.5 percentage points lower than that in 1990. On the contrary, due to a great number of rural migrant workers and by-business operators, the salary income is increasingly comprising a larger percentage of the rural resident's income. It was 30.2% in 2011, 16.2 percentage points higher than that in 1990. Table 3-3-2 and Table 3-3-3 show that, there is a big difference in transfer income in rural resident's income and urban resident's income. It reflects the difference in availability of social welfare to urban and rural residents.

Income Gap, Gini Coefficient and Off-payroll Income

The continuously widened income gap since the opening and opening-up policies were put into practice illustrates the indisputable fact of social polarization. For this, the gaps between urban and rural areas, different regions and different sectors are three major causes. In terms of the urban and rural gap, in 1985, the urban per capita disposable income was 1.8 times the rural per capita net income; by 2009, it had reached 3.33 times, hitting a historic high. A declining trend has occurred in recent years, for example, 3.23 times in 2010, and 3.13 times in 2011. In terms of the gap between different regions, in 2010, the urban resident's income was 1.7 times as much as the rural resident's income, and the northeastern part of China showed the lowest point; it was 2.45 times in the center of the country, 2.51 times in the east and 2.77 times in the west.

The Gini coefficient, ranging from 0 to 1, is a common indicator for measuring the gap between the income of different groups of residents. The higher the Gini coefficient , the larger the gap, while 0.4 is an internationally recognized warning line. Figure 3-3-2 shows the Gini coefficient of Chinese residents since 2003, which was published by the National Bureau of Statistics. It indicates that the Gini coefficient of China has been fluctuating closely near the warning line. Statistics by income level show that, there is still a large gap between the income of the high-income group and the low-income group. In 2010, in terms of urban residents, the ratio of per capita disposable income of the top 20%to that of the lowest 20% was 5.4:1; the ratio of per capita net income of the rural high-income group to that of the rural low-income group was 7.5:1, indicating that there is still a large gap between the high-income and low-income groups. Data of the Institute of Social Science Survey of Peking University on "Chinese Family Panel Survey" indicated that the per capita net income of each Chinese family in 2012 reached RMB 13,033. However, the per capita income of the 5% of families with the lowest income only reached RMB 1,000, and the per capita income of families under the 5% to 10% group only reached RMB 2,000, while the per capita income of the 5% of families with the highest income reached RMB 34,300. In terms of total family income, the income of

Figure 3-3-1
Trends of Absolute Growth in Income of Urban and Rural Residents

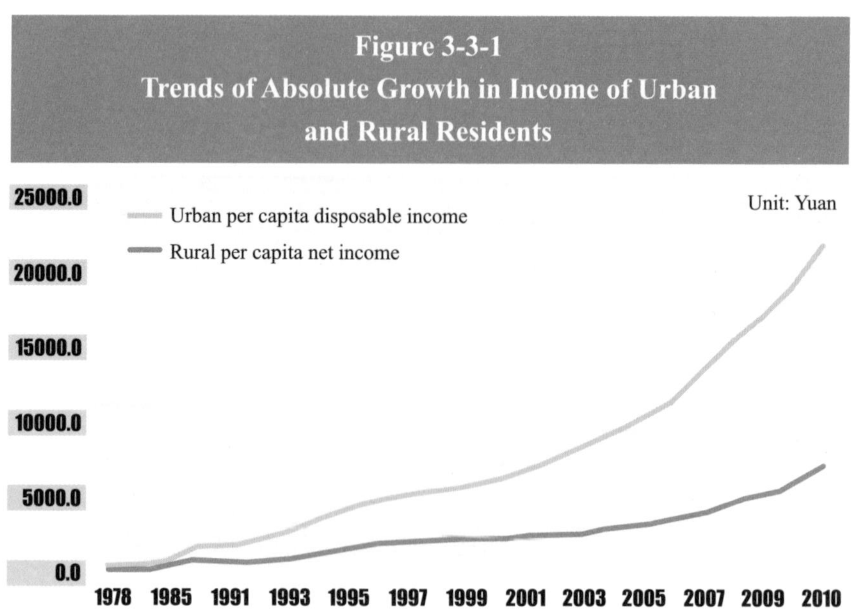

Figure 3-3-2
The Gini Coefficient of Chinese Residents Since 2003

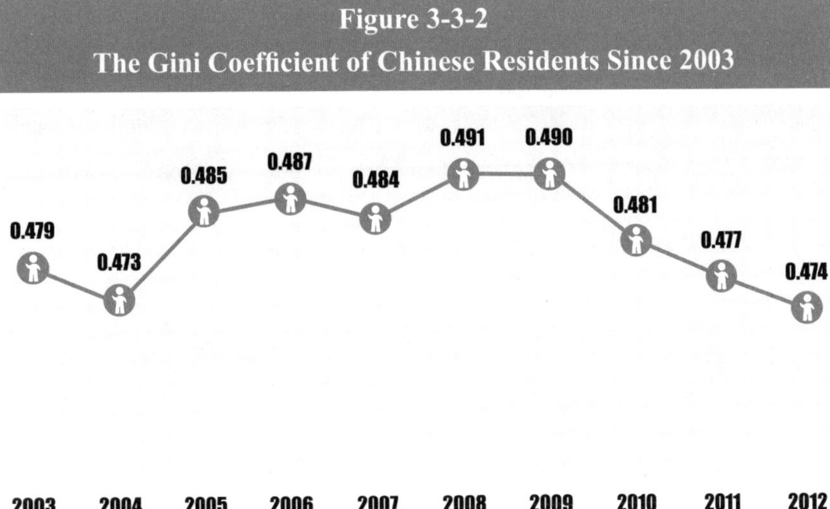

the 5% families with the lowest income accounted for 0.1% of the total income of all the families, and the income of the families under the 5% to 10% group accounted for 0.5%, while the income of the 5% of families with the highest income accounted for 23.4%. In addition, the income of families under the 90% to 94% group accounted for 11.75%; that of the 10% of families with the highest income accounted for 35.1%. the income of the 10% of families with the highest income was 58.5 times as much as that of the 10% of the families with the lowest income. The income of the 5% of families with the highest income was 234 times as much as that of the 5% of families with the lowest income. The national Gini coefficient in 2012 determined under the survey was 0.49, with a slight drop compared with that in 2010, but higher than that of the developed Western developed countries, Japan, ROK and other Asian countries and only a little bit lower than that of some Latin American and African countries (See Table 3-3-5). It should be noticed that, China is a big country with extremely unbalanced development in different regions and big income gaps, especially the gap between the eastern urban resident's income and the western rural resident's income. The people with the highest incomes mainly reside in the eastern metropolises, while

Table 3-3-4
The Gini Coefficient of Chinese Residents Since 2003
Unit: Yuan

Region	East	Central	West	Northeast
Annual average income of each rural family member	9233.16	6350.64	5604.05	9336.36
Annual average income of each urban family member	23153.21	15539.39	15523.05	15842.64
Per capita income of urban residents/ per capita income of rural residents	2.51	2.45	2.77	1.70

Table 3-3-5
Gini Coefficients of Some Countries

Country	Year	Gini Coefficient	Country	Year	Gini Coefficient
USA	2010	0.378	South Africa	2009	0.631
UK	2010	0.342	Brazil	2009	0.547
Japan	2010	0.329	Mexico	2008	0.483
Germany	2010	0.295	India	2005	0.334
France	2010	0.293	Malaysia	2009	0.462
Italy	2010	0.337	The Philippines	2009	0.430
ROK	2010	0.315	Egypt	2008	0.308
Russia	2009	0.401			

Data source: Database of the World Bank and database of OECD.

the people with the lowest incomes mainly reside in the western rural areas.

It should be also pointed out that, the actual income structure of China may be far more complicated than the official statistics, because, in addition to the incomes mentioned above, there are also off-payroll incomes, including welfare, off-payroll income from property, income from moonlighting ("grey income") and illegal income ("black income"). A study made by China Society of Economic Reform shows that off-payroll incomes mainly appear in urban areas, where social classes of higher ranking or with higher income tend to have more off-payroll incomes through more channels. Off-payroll incomes enlarge the Matthew Effect in polarization between the rich and the poor. The undeveloped financial market, fewer channels for individual investment and polarization between the rich and the poor leads to further polarization between the rich and the poor. On the other hand, off-payroll incomes also lead people to pursue unrealistic goals and provokes a hatred for wealthy people, and even

The examination of civil service has attracted much attention of the society. Usually, more than ten people compete for one job position.

a hatred for government officials due to some officials' corruption. In recent years, the number of people applying for the national public servant examination has increased, from more than 30,000 people in 2001 to more than 1.41 million people in 2011, an increase by a factor of 42 over 10 years. For four consecutive years, the number of qualified applicants for this examination each year exceeded one million. In 2012, 1.33 million people applied for the examination. The results of a survey show that, 65% of respondents said they wanted to be civil servant because of the stability of the jobs; 52% of respondents said it was because of the good payment and welfare; 34% of respondents said it was because of the high social status of civil servant; 27% of respondents said it was because of the faith to serve the country and the people; less than 20% of respondents said it was for further promotion. This is partly because it is hard for college students to find a job. Thus they compete for the "golden bowl". It also reflects the serious phenomenon of the official-oriented thought in China. Many people believe that the one who gains power gains benefits. This is why de-administration of state-owned enterprises and public institutions is being pushed forward. It is also the main cause of the conflict between the officials and the people. It is extremely urgent to solve the problem caused by off-payroll incomes, which is not just a problem concerning income distribution.

Social Organization Structure and Social Governance System

Social organization is an effective way to join the efforts of all social classes and circles. Under a market economy, government organization, social organization and market organization are the most basic forms of social organization. In China, due to a recent adoption of the system of market economy, the social organization structure still has some features of the traditional planned economy. Therefore, there is still a lot of work to do to improve the management and release the social vitality.

The Important Role of the Government

In China, the government plays an important role in resource allocation, while the function and potential of market mechanisms are restricted. Such an organization structure is helpful for "doing big things with limited resources". However, in many aspects, it does not fit the system of socialist market economy. There are serious problems, such as lack of distinction between the functions of the Party and those of the government, no separation between the government and the enterprises, excessive power of the government and excessively strict administration of the government, which not only restrict the market vitality and self-organization ability of the society, but also result in low efficiency of the government itself. In many cases, the government plays two roles, like the player and the referee in a football game. Therefore, it is hard to be absolutely fair and maintain a sound development of market. In addition, state-owned enterprises and public institutions maintain administrative status results in administrative operation of state-owned enterprises and public institutions and corporate governance (power marketization) of local governments. Therefore, not only the dominant role of state-owned enterprises and the development vitality of public institutions are weakened, but governmental functions may be abused.

In recent years, the Chinese government has been attempting reform of the government management system in relevant fields. The general guideline for this is to transform the function of the government, establish a service-oriented government, rule the country by law, and separate the functions of the government for those of enterprises, public institutions and society. At the end of 2013, the Third Plenary Session of the 18th Central Committee of the CPC adopted the *Decision on Major Issues Concerning Comprehensively Deepening Reforms*, which proposed to evolve the decisive role of the market in resource allocation, streamline government structure and perform government duties comprehensively and correctly. In details, great efforts should made to further deepen the reform of administrative review and approval procedures, and

The transformation of government roles was one of the important issues of "China Reform Forum in 2013" in Beijing.

reduce the central government's control over market operations to a minimal level. The government should cancel all administrative approval procedures for economic activities under the effective regulation of the market mechanism, and should manage matters that require administrative approval according to procedures and with high efficiency. The government should transfer large-scale and high-participation social and economic projects to local and community-level management for convenience and efficiency. The government should strengthen the formulation and implementation of development strategies, plans, policies and standards, enhance market activity monitoring and supply of public services, enhance the central government's competence in macro control, and improve local governments' performance in public services, market supervision, social management and environmental protection. It will promote government purchases of public services by means of contract and entrustment, and introduce a competition mechanism into general-affairs management services.

The macro-control of Chinese government has proved to be highly successful for its decentralization.

In 1988, the citizens queued to buy eggs in Shengli Road of Luoyang City, Henan Province during the period of planned economy.

Features of the Unit System

Under the system of planned economy, the Chinese people worked and lived based on "units", which shouldered all responsibilities for their employees, such as their livelihood, health care and pension. Therefore, these units, whether referring to government organizations, public institutions, factories, mines or people's communes, were society. However, since the reform and opening-up, the social structure has greatly changed, and "people relying on units" are changing into "social beings", though there is still a long way to go. For example, there are still strong administrative elements in the management of public institutions, and the responsibilities and restrictions of the units are in direct proportion to the administrative resources owned by the "units". The Third Plenary Session of the 18th Central Committee of the CPC proposed to accelerate the reform of public institutions based on the classification of their functions, increase government purchases of public services, straighten out the relationship between public institutions and their competent administrative departments, and promote de-administration of public institutions. Meanwhile, the government will create conditions to gradually rescind the administrative ranks of schools, research institutes and hospitals, and will set up legal person governance structures for public institutions, transform qualified public institutions into enterprises or social organizations, and establish a unified registration system for the management of public institutions of all kinds. De-administration of state-owned enterprises will be made gradually.

A Social Organization Structure in Need of Further Improvement and Showing a Good Development Trend

Table 3-4-1 shows, according to the official classification, public management and social organizations are divided into five categories: CPC organizations; national organs; the CPPCC and democratic parties; the mass organizations, social groups and religious organizations; the grassroots mass self-governing organizations. The first three categories are public management organizations, while the fifth category is that of mass self-governing organizations. The organizations under the fourth category are more like social organizations. Actually, China had no "social organizations" in the past. Under the planned economy, there were no non-government or non-official organizations except for "social groups". In 1986, the name of the "Department of Social Groups Management" of the Ministry of Civil Affairs was changed into the "Bureau of Civil Organizations", which enabled the civil organizations to have legal status. The same year, the State Council issued the amended *Regulation on Registration and Administration of Social Organizations and the Regulation on Management of Non-enterprise Civil Organizations*, setting up the model of departments of civil affairs responsible for registration while the Party and government administration departments are responsible for daily management.

In 2006, when the Sixth Plenary Session of the 16th Central Committee of the CPC was held, the term of "civil organization" was officially changed into "social organization"to avoid misunderstanding of the relationship between the roles of the government and the people under traditional political and social orders, and these traditional "civil organizations" were made participants in the overall innovative social management and construction of a harmonious society. The use of the term of "social organization" enables all sectors of society to have correct understanding of such organizations and encourage them to pay attention to and support such organizations. It keeps in line with the trend of rapid development of such organizations in these years.

China has three types of social organizations, including social groups, foundations and private non-enterprise units. Social groups are established by citizens, enterprises or public institutions on a voluntary basis, including

At the end of 2013, the head of State-owned Assets Supervision and Administration Commission of the State Council indicated in the press conference that they would explore and establish the differentiated salary distribution system of the managers in state-owned enterprises.

Table 3-4-1
Public Management and Social Organizations of China

Code				Type
Category	Subcategory	Class	Subclass	
S				Public management and social organizations
	93			CPC organizations
		930	9300	CPC organizations
	94			National organs
		941	9410	National organs of power
		942		National administrative organs
			9421	Comprehensive affairs management organs
			9422	Foreign affairs management organs
			9423	Public security management organs
			9424	Social affairs management organs
			9425	Economic affairs management organs
			9426	Government affairs management organs
			9427	Administrative supervision and inspection organs
		943		People's court and people's procuratorate
			9431	People's court
			9432	People's procuratorate
		949	9490	Other national organs
	95			CPPCC and democratic parties
		951	9510	CPPCC
		952	9520	Democratic parties

Section	Division	Group	Class	Category
S				Public management and social organizations
	96			Mass organizations, social groups and religious organizations
		961		Mass organizations
			9611	Trade unions
			9612	The Women's Federation
			9613	The Communist Youth League
			9619	Other mass organizations
		962		Social groups
			9621	Professional groups
			9622	Industrial groups
			9629	Other social groups
		963	9630	Religious organizations
	97			Grassroots mass self-governing organizations
		971	9710	Community self-governing organizations
		972	9720	Village self-governing organizations

industrial groups, academic groups, professional groups and united groups. Foundations are social organizations engaged in public welfare undertakings by using donated assets, and include public foundations and non-public foundations. Private non-enterprise units are social organizations established by enterprises or public institutions, social groups or other social forces or individuals with non-state-owned assets for social service activities. Such units are divided into ten categories, including education, health, science and technology, culture, labor, civil administration, sports, intermediary services and legal services. The statistics of the Ministry of Civil Affairs showed that by the end of 2012, China had 499,000 social organizations, up 8.1% over the previous year. These organizations provided jobs for 6.133 million people, up 2.3% over the previous year. They generated a total of fixed assets of RMB 142.54 billion. The added value of social organizations reached RMB 52.56 billion, down 20.4% over the previous year, accounting for 0.23% of the added value of the tertiary industry. In detail, there were 271,000 social groups, up 6.3% over the previous year. Of these groups, 27,056 were industrial and business service groups; 18,486 were scientific and technical research groups; 11,654 were education groups; 10,440 were health groups; 38,381 were social service groups; 25,036 were cultural groups; 15,060 were sports groups; 6,816 were ecological environment groups; 3,191 were legal groups; 4,693 were religious groups; 55,383 were agricultural and rural development groups; 18,611 were occupation and employment organizations; 499 were international and other foreign-related organizations; 35,825 groups of other types. At the same time, China had 3,029 foundations, increasing by 415 (15.9%) compared with that of the previous year, with a growth of 15.9%. Of them, there were 1,316 public foundations, 1,686 non-public foundations, eight foreign-related foundations, and 19 overseas representative organizations of foundations. There were 199 foundations with registration at the Ministry of Civil Affairs. The public foundations and non-public foundations received RMB 30.57 billion of donations from all sectors of society. In addition, China had 225,000 private non-enterprise units, up 10.1% over the previous year. Of them, there were 11,126 science and technology service units, 1,065 ecological environment units, 117,015 education units, 20,979 health units, 35,956 social service units, 10,590 cultural units, 8,490 sports units, 8,717 business service units, 132 religious units, 49 international and other foreign-related organizations, and 10,989 units of other types. Please refer to Figure 3-4-1 and Table 3-4-2 for the development trends of social organizations .

Social organizations play a role in social governance that cannot be replaced by the government or units. As concluded in the *Outline of the Twelfth Five-Year Plan for National Economic and Social Development* of the Chinese government, social organizations have three functions: providing services, reflecting appeals

Figure 3-4-1
Development Trends of Social Organizations for Nearly a Decade

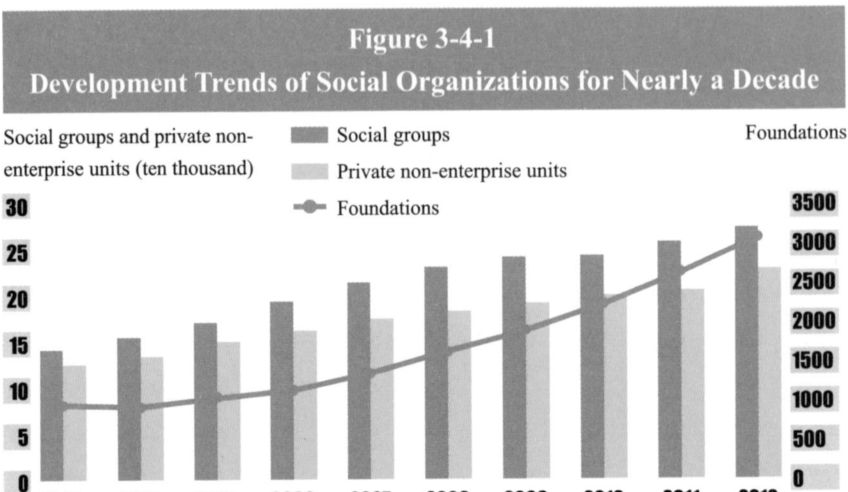

Table 3-4-2
Statistics on Development of Social Organizations Since 2005

Indicator	2005	2006	2007	2008	2009	2010	2011	2012
Social groups	17.1	19.2	21.2	23	23.9	24.5	25.5	27.1
Foundation	975	1144	1340	1579	1843	2200	2614	3029
Private non-enterprise units	14.8	16.1	17.4	18.2	19	19.8	20.4	22.5

and normalizing behavior. In addition, the outline also included specific plans for the development of social organizations, including improving management of social organizations and establishing a social organization management system featuring unified registration, clearly designated functions, coordination and cooperation, responsibilities by levels, and supervision by law; focusing on and give priority to the development of economic organizations, public-benefit and charity organizations, private non-enterprise units and urban and rural community organizations; promoting reform and development of industrial associations and chambers of commerce, enhancing industrial self-regulation and giving full play to the function of social organizations for the communication between the government and enterprises; improving support policies, promoting function transformation from government departments to social organizations, making more public resources available to social organizations, and expanding types and scope of tax preference.

Currently, the problem is that, due to historical reasons, many non-government organizations are being managed mostly in an administrative way. A lot of social groups were established by the government, and some industrial associations and chambers of commerce also derived from government departments and still have some administrative functions. This results in too much intervention of government in social organizations and lack of conditions for social organizations to seek independent development. The Third Plenary Session of the 18th Central Committee of the CPC proposed to "correctly handle the relationship between the government and society, intensify efforts to separate government administration and social organizations, encourage social organizations to clarify their rights and obligations, and enforce self-management and play their role in accordance with the law"; "commission social organizations to provide public services that they are apt to supply and tackle matters that they are able to tackle"; and "achieve a true disconnection of trade associations and chambers of commerce from administrative departments". This will be helpful for the de-administration of some social organizations to strengthen their independence and vitality.

Grassroots Self-governing in Need of Further Improvement

The grassroots self-governing organizations of China mainly include neighborhood committees and residents' groups in urban area as well as village committees and villagers' groups in rural areas. As the mass self-governing organizations in urban areas, neighborhood committees originated in the

early years after the founding of the New China. In 1954, the *Regulations on Organization of Urban Neighborhood Committees* was issued. It was the first law on neighborhood committees, specifying the nature, status and functions of neighborhood committees. Then, after experiencing a winding course for decades, neighborhood committees had achieved all-around development after the reform and opening-up policies were put into practice. In January 1980, the Standing Committee of the National People's Congress adopted and issued the *Regulations on Organization of Neighborhood Committees*, the *Interim General Rules on People's Mediation Committee, and the Interim General Rules on Public Security Committee*. In 1982, for the first time, the nature, mission and function of neighborhood committees were written into the Constitution of the People's Republic of China, the fundamental law of China. Afterward, related rectifications and standardization were made for organization of neighborhood committees based on the law. To fully guarantee self-governance and the

The general election of the communities in Nanjing on Oct. 13th, 2012. People voted for their "head".

democratic rights of the urban residents, and after years of study and analysis of the experiences and lessons from the implementation of the *Regulations on Organization of Neighborhood Committees* , the 11th Conference of the Standing Committee of the National People's Congress held on December 26, 1989, adopted the *Law on Organization of Urban Neighborhood Committees*, showing that the organization of urban neighborhood committees had entered a new stage of comprehensive development.

Village committees were established later, in early 1980s. In 1982, when drafting amendments to the constitution, the Standing Committee of the National People's Congress took lessons from the operation of urban neighborhood committees and the experiences of the rural residents and made specific regulations on the nature and missions of village committees, and clarified principles for the organization of village committees. Based on that, township governments were established based on original people's communes in many areas, while village committees and villagers' groups were established based on production brigades. In 1998 China formally issued the *Law on Organization of Village Committees*. In 2010 the law was amended to reflect new conditions and trends. Since then, the grassroots self-governing organizations in rural areas have experienced fast development. By the end of 2012, China had680,000 grassroots self-governing organizations, including 588,000 village committees, 4.694 million villages' groups and 2.323 million committee members; 91,153 neighborhood committees, 1.335 million residents' groups and 469,000 committee members. Please refer to Figure 3-4-2 and Table 3-4-3 for the tendency of the development of the grassroots self-governing organizations. It shows that, along with urbanization, the development of village committees was inversely proportional to the development of neighborhood committees.

In addition to neighborhood committees and village committees, grassroots self-governing organizations also include democratic management organizations of enterprise staff, or workers' representative conferences. The system of

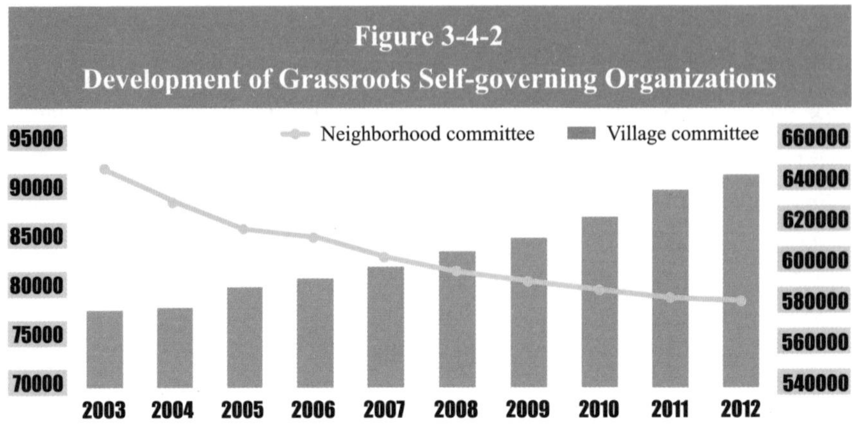

Figure 3-4-2
Development of Grassroots Self-governing Organizations

Table 3-4-3
Development of Grassroots Self-governing Organizations in China

Indicator	2005	2006	2007	2008	2009	2010	2011	2012
Neighborhood committee	79947	80717	82006	83413	84689	87057	89480	91153
Village committee	629079	623669	612709	604285	599078	594658	589653	588475

workers' representative conferences was first established in the 1950s, and then deserted during the Cultural Revolution and reestablished in early 1980s. In 1986, *The Regulations on Representative Conferences of Workers in Industrial Enterprises Owned by the Whole People* was issued. In 1988, it was the first time that the system of workers' representative conferences was made a part of state law, namely the *Law of the People's Republic of China on Industrial Enterprises Owned by the Whole People*. As specified, the workers' representative conference has the following functions: to hear and deliberate enterprise operations, development plans and programs and put forward opinions and suggestions; to examine and endorse or reject the enterprise's programs for wage adjustment, programs for bonus distribution, measures for labor protection, measures for awards and penalties and other important rules and regulations; to deliberate and decide on the programs for the use of the staff and workers' welfare fund, programs for allocation of the staff and workers' housing and other important matters concerning the well-being and benefits of the staff and workers; to evaluate and supervise the leading administrative cadres at various levels of the enterprise and put forward suggestions for rewarding or punishing them and for their appointment or removal; and to recommend and elect factory directors. After the workers' representative conference is closed, the Trade Union Committee of an enterprise shall take the responsibilities for the daily work of the workers' representative conference. Since 1998, the system for transparent enterprise (factory) operation was adopted in state-owned enterprises, collectively-owned enterprises and other holding companies, and then extended to non-public enterprises. In October 2001, the amended *Trade Union Law of the People's Republic of China* was issued to further guarantee the function of the workers' representative conference as one of the mechanisms of trade unions to protect the legitimate rights and interests of employees. During the development process, many enterprises, public institutions and organs and units have, based upon their own characteristics, established a new democratic management pattern, which is based on the workers' representative conference and supplemented by the system for transparent enterprise (factory) operation, labor contract system, the system of consultation on the basis of equality and the collective contract system, the collective wage negotiation system, and the worker director (supervisor) system. Until 2010, 2.113 million enterprises and public institutions had adopted the system for transparent enterprise (factory) operation, and 2.249 million had established the system of workers' representative conference.

All forms of grassroots mass self-governing organizations, including the urban neighborhood committees, rural village committees, workers' representative conferences of enterprises and public institutions, the representative conference of residents (members), consultation committees, property owner committees,

The old offices of village committee in Guoliang Village, Huxian County, Henan Province.

resident appraisal committees, hearing, non-government organizations and volunteer organizations of urban communities, as well as the villagers' conferences or the villager representatives' conferences, villagers' groups, villagers' financial groups and the transparent village administration supervision groups, make up the most direct and widest democratic practices. Since the 17th National Congress of the CPC, they have been recognized as political systems with Chinese characteristics together with the system of the people's congress, the system of multi-party cooperation and political consultations led by the CPC and the system of regional autonomy of ethnic minorities. Since the new century began, the Chinese government has made great efforts to build harmonious communities and a new socialist countryside. This provides opportunities for a prosperous development of grassroots self-governing organizations. However, generally speaking, the development of the grassroots mass self-governing and community service system of China is still in an initial stage, with certain difficulties and problems, including: unclear definition of authority and responsibilities of grassroots mass self-governing organizations and grassroots Party organizations and superior governments, resulting in excessive administrative intervention; lack of participation of grassroots masses, resulting in lack of workers, unsatisfied treatment and low motivation for work; and lack of attention to grassroots mass self-governing organizations, resulting in insufficient service facilities, lack of unified planning, low guarantee capability, limited self-governing capability, strong dependence on administrative resources and difficulties in creating a positive circle; canvassing and bribery at election in some rural areas, resulting in village affairs being controlled by certain families with strong power. Since the 17th National Congress of the CPC, the Chinese government has tried to solve these problems from many aspects, including system establishment, organization development, democratic election practices, decision-making, management and supervision and establishment of guarantee mechanism. The *Outline of the Twelfth Five-Year Plan for National Economic*

In 2014, the proposal of the All-China Federation of Trade Union suggested the concerns about the cultural construction of the new generations of migrant workers.

and Social Development issued in 2011 included a chapter on plans to enhance community self-governing and service functions by improving community governance structures and establishing community management and service platforms, with emphasis on talent development and service capacity building. The Third Plenary Session of the 18th Central Committee of the CPC shifted the focus from social management to social governance, reflecting the expectations of the ruling party for the participation of enterprises, social organizations and grassroots mass self-governing organizations in social governance.

Unique Functions of Party Organizations at the Primary Level

In the social organization structure of China, there is a unique component that should not be neglected, namely the Party organizations at the primary level. To enable the Party's organization foundation is well-connected with social organizations, the basic organization of the CPC consists of production units and work units. Such principles have been followed since the revolutionary period. According to the statistics of the Organization Department of the CPC Central Committee, by 2012, there have been 85.127 million CPC members and 4.201 million Party organizations at the primary level. A total of 7,245 urban subdistricts, 33,000 towns, 87,000 communities (neighborhood committees) and 588,000 villages had established Party organizations. Meanwhile, 99.97% of enterprises and 99.4% of public institutions had established Party organizations. In addition, 99.98% of public enterprises and 99.95% (1.475 million) of non-public enterprises with sufficient conditions for establishing Party organizations had established Party organizations. A total of 40,300 social groups had established Party organizations, accounting for 99.21% of social groups with sufficient conditions for establishing such organizations; and 39,500 private non-enterprise units had established Party organizations, accounting for 99.61% of private non-enterprise units with sufficient conditions for establishing such organizations.

Thanks to the Party organizations at the primary level, which serve as a "bridge" and "link" between the grassroots and the Party, the Party has gained the biggest advantage for maintaining close ties with the masses. Entering the new century, the CPC and the Chinese government have been keeping pace with the times, further highlighting the task of social construction. They have laid the emphasis on social security and improvement of people's livelihoods. At the same time, the Party organizations at the primary level that play an important role in social construction and management are attracting more and more attention. The Fourth Plenary Session of the 16th Central Committee of the CPC first proposed to "build and improve the social management model featuring leadership of the Party committees, accountability of governments, social cooperation and the public participation". The political reports of the 17th National Congress of the CPC and the 18th National Congress of the CPC made a conclusion of the functions of the Party organizations at the primary level: promoting development,

On Apr, 18th, 2011, the new party committee of villages and towns was elected through acclamation and direct election in the party congress of Liucheng County, Liuzhou City, Guangxi Province. The picture shows that the staff counted the votes of the candidates.

serving the people, rallying public support and promoting harmony, reflecting the needs of the time for the participation of the Party organizations at the primary level in social construction and governance. It is proved that the Party organizations at the primary level serve as the first "defensive line" for maintaining social stability, a supporting point for the Party to rally public support and a core force for promoting development and improving people's livelihoods. To give full play to these functions, it is important to meet the requirements of the development trends and tasks and carry out activities in an innovative way. In detail, it requires consistency with the overall requirements for building a service-oriented Party -- the Party's aim and the nature of Party organizations -- so as to make full use of the advantage of maintaining close ties with the masses and making Party organizations at the primary level more service-oriented, with serving the people and engaging in people-related work being their main tasks.

On Mar 28th, 2013, a special enlarged meeting was convened in a poverty-stricken family by the party committee of Letianxi Town, Yiling District, Yichang City, Hubei Province, deliberating solutions of some issues, such as the reconstruction of dilapidated houses, medical assistance, education and employment of children, spring ploughing, etc.

In recent years, there have been many typical cases. For example, Shanghai established the regional Party building platform, which is used to promote the development of social organizations under the support of the Party organizations. Responding to the call for construction of new economic organizations and social organizations, the platform aims to effectively integrate the building of the Party organizations at primary level to the grassroots social governance. This reflects the function of the Party organizations at the primary level in the grassroots social governance. Beijing has adopted the community-based system consisting of Party organization, neighborhood committee and service station, which have clearly assigned missions and complementary functions. There are also numerous examples in rural areas, which are based on system and mechanism construction to allow the Party organizations at the primary level to play a more important role in rural social governance and economic development. Of course, while making a number of remarkable achievements in foundation and grassroots construction, many areas are facing difficulties and bottlenecks. Therefore, greater efforts should be made to further improve related mechanism, make innovations, raise awareness and promote foundation and grassroots construction.

Notes

16. For more details, please refer to *Analysis on Economic Consequences of Lagged Urbanization* by Li Wen, *Social Science in China*, Volume 4, 2001; *Conclusion and Assessment on China's Urbanization Over Approximately Half A Century, Study on Contemporary History of China*, Volume 4, 2002
17. *Change of China's Social Stratification Structure in 60 Years*, by Lu Xueyi, Journal of Beijing University of Technology, Volume 3, 2010

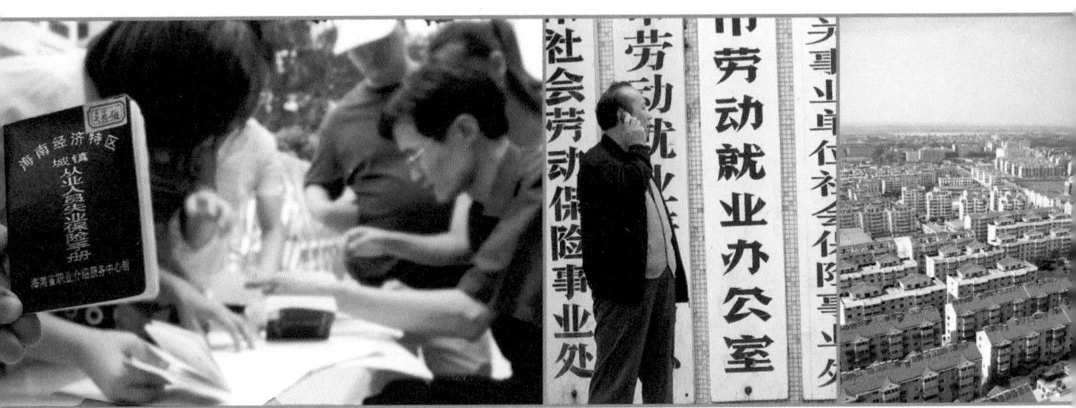
海南经济特区
城镇
从业人员失业保险手册
社会劳动保险事业处
市劳动就业办公室

The world's Largest Social Security Scheme

Setting up a sound social security system is an important way and systematical arrangement to regulate social differentiation and protect fairness and justice. Since the reform and opening up policy was implemented, especially in this century, China's social security undertakings have developed rapidly. At present, China has set up a framework with wide coverage and complete programs for the social security system with social insurance, social relief and social welfare as the foundation and basic pension, medical insurance and minimum subsistence guarantee system as the key content. The world's largest social security scheme has been established. The 12th Five-Year Plan period (2011-2015) is the critical period of building a well-off society, the crucial period to accelerate transformation of the economic development model and maintain the steady and rapid economic development and an important period to deepen the social security reform and realize breakthroughs in key junctures.

Basic Situation of the Development of Social Security Before this Century

The Social Security System in the Planned Economy Period

The social security system of New China was set up with the labor insurance system as its core. As early as 1951, China formulated and promulgated the *Labor Insurance Regulations of the People's Republic of China* which was implemented in state-owned enterprises, enterprises under the public-private partnership, private enterprises and enterprises of cooperatives ownership which had more than 100 employees. According to the regulations, the items covered by the labor insurance included: medical treatment, work-related injury, diseases, non-work related injury, maternity, work-related disability and disease, non-work related disability, pension, work-related death and disease, non-work related death, medical subsidy to the immediate family of employees, funeral subsidy, etc. In 1953, the Government Administration Council amended the Regulation to expand the coverage to the basic construction units of industry and mining and transportation enterprises and state-owned construction enterprises with improved treatment standards, although the number of items was not changed. The central government promoted the *Labor Insurance Regulations* in all the state-owned enterprises when socialist renovation was completed for all handicrafts under the individual ownership and private businesses around 1956. Some large enterprises of collective ownership with good economic conditions also exercised or referred to the regulations. In the same period, the social security system for the workers of the state organs and institutional units was gradually set up, with the same item coverage with the *Labor Insurance Regulations*, and slightly higher treatment standards. The State Council amended the *Labor Insurance Regulations* in 1958 and 1978, upon approval from the Standing Committee of the National People's Congress, and improved treatment standards. The employee retirement plan was enacted as an independent order.

The vast rural area exercised the Five Guarantees (food, clothing, medical treatment and funeral) system to the special groups relying on the collective economy. The household that enjoyed the Five Guarantees was named "five guarantee household". The 1956–1967 *Outline for the National Agricultural Development* (amended draft) clearly set forth: "The rural cooperatives shall designate production groups or teams to make unified and proper arrangements

The old workers at the port of Dalian filled the cards of labor insurance in the early 1950s.

With the reform of economic system, the social security system in China has been under reconstruction.

in production to the cooperative members who have no kin and cannot support themselves; and offer proper care to them to ensure food, clothing, fuel, education (children) and funeral services." That was the early form of the "five-guarantee" system of the rural area with Chinese characteristics. Since the 1950s, the elderly homes were set up in various areas to take care of some of the Five-Guarantee households in a centralized way and a Five-Guarantee support system gradually took shape with both centralized and dispersed support forms. In the early 1960s, the content of Five Guarantees was changed from food, clothing, fuel, education and funeral to food, clothing, housing, medical treatment and funeral (education, for orphans only). In the early days of reform when the production responsibility system was implemented, the support form and supply channels were changed, but the treatment remained unchanged.

In terms of the medical guarantee, cadres (employees of the stage organs and institutional units) and enterprise employees were basically supported by the public-funded medical system while the mutual-assistance cooperative medical system was implemented for farmers. As for the housing guarantee, in the rural area farmers basically lived in the self-built houses (special care was offered to the Five-Guarantee Households) while the urban residents lived in the houses allocated by the government or units, free of charge. In addition, a social security and administrative welfare system was set up for special groups (servicemen, families of the revolutionary martyrs and servicemen and orphans, the elderly,

Figure 4-1-1
Structure of China's Social Security System in the Planned Economy Period

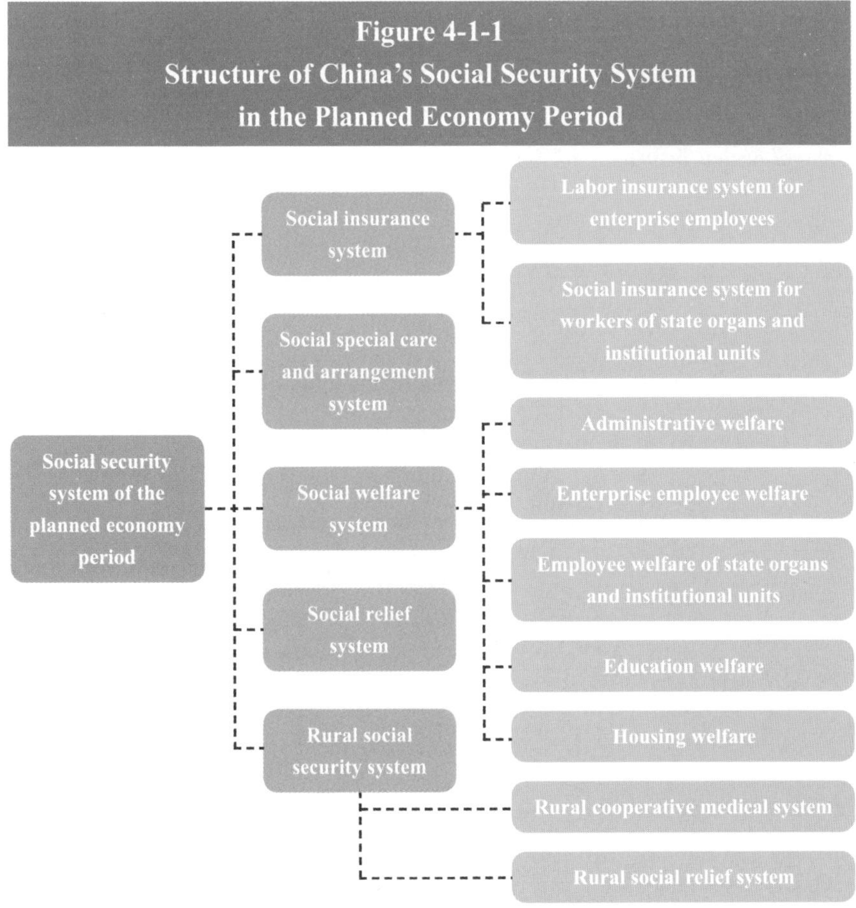

disabled in urban areas). Generally, the social security was unsound, with small coverage and a relatively low guarantee level, but it was appropriate for the economic level, economic system and social administrative system of that time and played an active role in economic and social development.

Matching System Reconstruction to the State-owned Enterprise Reform

The reconstruction of the social security system in the new period was rolled out accompanying the economic system reform, especially the state-owned enterprise reform. The *Interim Provisions on Implementing the Labor Contract System in State-owned Enterprises* promulgated by the State Council in 1986 was an important symbol of the transformation from the traditional retirement system to the unemployment insurance system. The *Interim Provisions on Unemployment Insurance of Employees of State-owned Enterprises* promulgated in the same year unveiled the reconstruction of China's unemployment insurance system and reflected the socialization tendency of the reform of social security system. In the same period, the traditional public-funded medical system was improved. In the middle and late 1990s, the social insurance system reform accelerated to adapt to the requirements of the state-owned enterprise reform. The State Council released the *Circular on Deepening Reform of the Enterprise Employee Pension System* in 1995 and two implementation measures as attachment, indicating the launch of the pension system with contributions from both social pooling funds and individual accounts. Two years later, the State Council released the *Decisions on Setting up a Unified Basic Pension System for Enterprise Employees* and consequently the plans for contributions from both the social pooling funds and individual accounts were to be unified. In order to ensure implementation of the enterprise employment system reform, the central government set up "three guarantee measures" to make up for insufficiency of unemployment relief: the unemployment service center guaranteed the basic

A management center for medical insurance affairs in a district of Beijing.

livelihood of the laid-off employees; those who failed to get a job after three years of registration with the unemployment service center would be transferred to the social insurance institutions to get unemployment benefits; those who could not find a job after two years of receiving the unemployment benefits would be transferred to the civil administration departments to enjoy the minimum subsistence allowance of urban residents. Meanwhile, China attempted to set up a medical insurance system with diversified forms in line with the same thinking. The promulgation of the *Unemployment Insurance Regulations* in 1999 was an important step to improve the unemployment insurance system. Thus an embryo of the enterprise employee social insurance framework was framed, with pension, medical insurance and unemployment insurance as the key content.

In the first several years of the new century, China's social security system reform proceeded following the track designated in the previous stage. The experiences were summarized from time to time to ensure that the basic pension of laid-off employees and retirees of state-owned enterprises was paid

The unemployed received unemployment insurance benefits.

on time and the insurance system reform was promoted steadily. The livelihood guarantee system of laid-off employees of state-owned enterprises was basically integrated into the unemployment insurance system. The coverage of the social insurance system was enlarged continuously with improved guarantee capacity. By the end of the 10th Five-Year Plan period (2001–2005), the systems of basic pension insurance, basic medical insurance, unemployment insurance, work-related injury insurance and maternity insurance covered 175 million, 138 million, 106 million, 84.78 million, 54.08 million people, respectively. A total of 54.42 million of farmers were covered by the rural pension insurance system. In 2005, the revenues and expenses of the social security funds were RMB 696.8 billion and RMB 540.1 billion, respectively. In the same period, progresses had been made in the socialized management services for enterprise retirees and the occupational pension system rolled out. The social security system reform in this period made important contributions to the state-owned enterprise reform and economic structure adjustment.

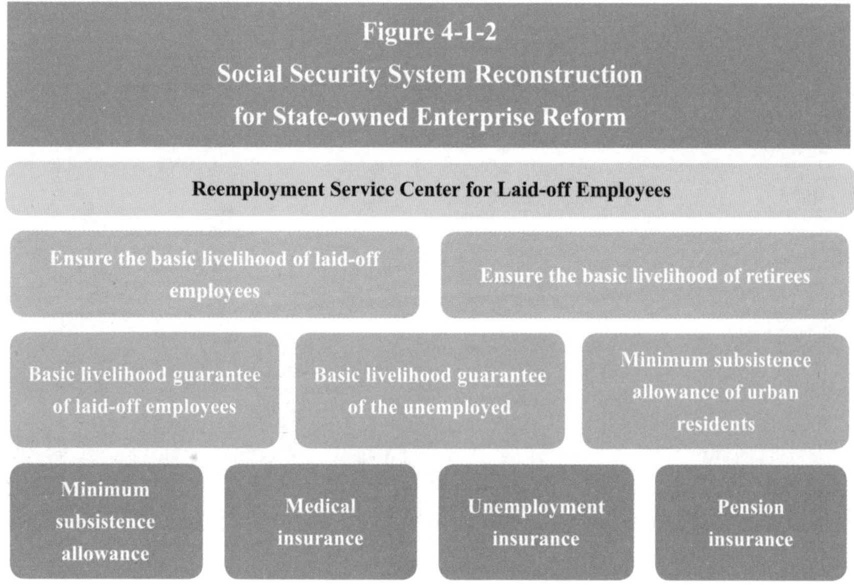

Social Security System-building Accelerated in an All-round Way

From the aspect of the new situation, new missions and new characteristics of economic and social development, the Chinese government put forward the important strategic thinking of a scientific outlook on development and the important strategic mission of building a harmonious socialist society, and promulgated a series of policies and measures of great significance to the direct interests of the people in the past ten-plus years. The social security system attracted unprecedented attention as a basic program of the livelihood policies and embarked on a fast track of urban-rural coordination with wide coverage of all of society.

As the core of social security system, social insurance has aroused people's attention.

Social Insurance

Social insurance is an integral part of the social security system. In recent years, the Chinese government has promulgated the *Social Insurance Law of the People's Republic of China and amended the Work-related Injury Insurance Regulations*. Efforts have been made to set up a new rural pension insurance system and implement pilot programs in various areas, set up a provincial pooling system for the basic pension insurance system of enterprise employees, establish and implement the basic medical insurance system for urban residents, the new rural cooperative medical care insurance and urban-rural medical relief system widely, and further improve the basic medical insurance system for workers. Good results have been achieved, especially with the practice of including migrant workers in the basic pension system of urban employees in the beginning of 2009, and in pilot programs of new rural pension insurance launched at the end of 2009 and urban resident pension insurance launched in

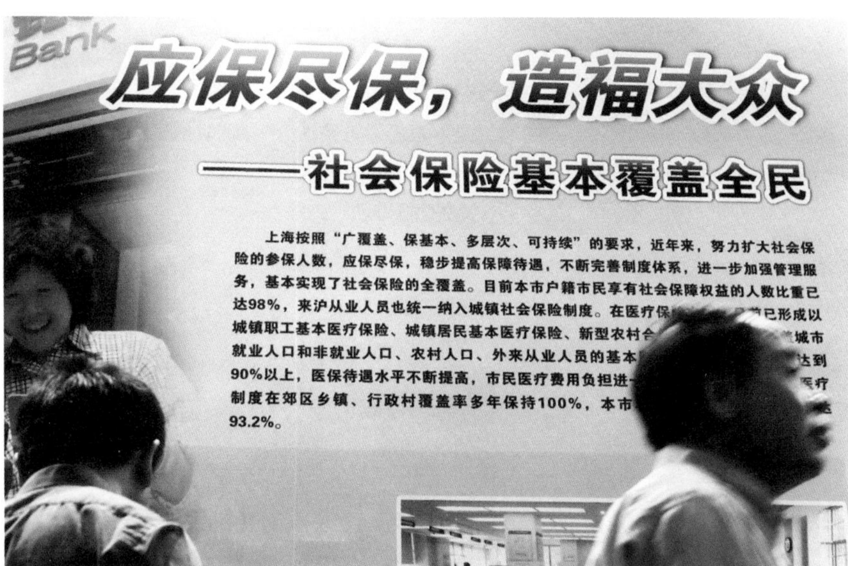

The idea has been widely spread that social insurance is almost universal in China.

July 2011. In 2012, these systems achieved full coverage of the target groups. By the end of 2013, the new rural pension insurance system and the urban resident pension insurance system covered 498 million persons, of which 138 million were receiving benefits. With employee pension insurance, a total of 820 million of people are covered by the social insurance system.

In February 2014, the State Council distributed the *Opinions on Establishing a Unified Basic Pension System for Urban and Rural Residents* and moved to set up a unified basic pension system and integrate the new rural pension system with the urban pension system by the end of the 12th Five-Year Plan period to set up a fair, unified and standard urban-rural resident pension system that is consistent with the social relief, social welfare and other social security policies before 2020. In this way, the home care and other traditional elderly care models will be given full play to guarantee the basic livelihood of the elderly in a better way. The *2013 National Economic and Social Development Statistics Bulletin*

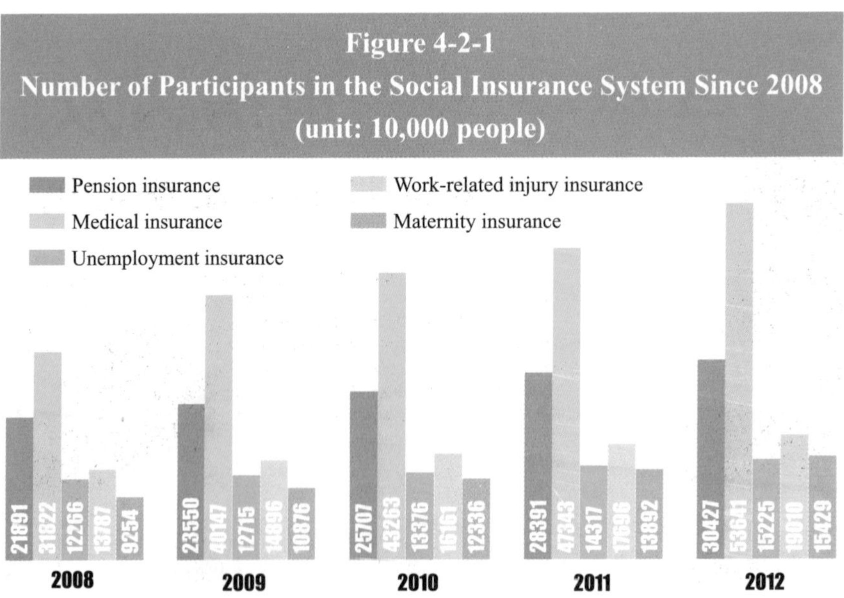

Figure 4-2-1
Number of Participants in the Social Insurance System Since 2008
(unit: 10,000 people)

Data source: Ministry of Human Resources and Social Security, *2012 Statistical Bulletin on Human Resources and Social Security Development.*

released by the National Bureau of Statistics in February 2014 show that by the end of 2013, 322.12 million citizens were covered by the urban employee pension system, 497.50 million were covered by the basic urban-rural pension insurance system and 573.22 million by the basic medical insurance system. Of that, the participants of the employee medical insurance system totaled 274.16 million and the participants of resident medical insurance totaled 299.06 million. The unemployment insurance system had 164.17 million participants and 1.97 million receiving unemployment benefits. The work-related insurance system had 198.97 million participants, including 72.66 million migrant workers. The maternity insurance system had 163.97 million participants. A total of 2,489 counties, cities and districts implemented the new rural cooperative medical insurance system, with a participation rate of 99.0%. Calculating at the poverty-relief standards of per capita annual net income of 2,300 yuan (2010, fixed price), the poverty-stricken population in rural areas in 2013 was 82.49 million, a decrease of 16.50 million.

Social Relief

In this period, China gave priority to establishing and improving emergency plans and the early warning system to cope with abrupt public events while enforcing the social relief system. The *Regulations of Minimum Subsistence Allowance for Urban Residents* was promulgated in 1999, the *Circular of the State Council on Establishing the Minimum Subsistence Allowance System in the Rural Area* was promulgated in August 2007 to set up the rural minimum subsistence allowance system and pay the subsistence allowance in full to beneficiaries on time. In that year, 2,777 agriculture-related counties, cities and districts) of the 31 provinces, autonomous regions and municipalities had set up the rural minimum subsistence allowance system. The establishment of the urban minimum subsistence allowance system set off the defects of the traditional social relief system from the root and laid a foundation for integration of urban and rural social relief. Meanwhile, with more beneficiaries of the social relief system and gradual increase of the relief standards and relief benefits, the relief procedures have been standardized gradually to guarantee the livelihood of needy people.

In the same period, the Central Committee of the CPC and the State Council released orders to offer medical relief to poverty-stricken farmers in 1997 and 2002 to ensure meeting the basic medical requirements of needy people. In 2003, the Ministry of Civil Affairs and other departments jointly issued the *Opinions on Implementing Medical Relief in Rural Areas* to establish a medical relief system in rural areas. In 2005, the General Office of the State Council distributed the *Opinions on Pilot Programs of Urban Medical Relief System* jointly formulated by the Ministry of Civil Affairs and other ministries. In 2008, the urban medical relief system was rolled out through pilot programs and the rural medical relief system was further improved. A medical relief system was set up with full coverage of the whole country with a relief mode combining both the direct relief and assistance in insurance participation. In 2009 and 2012, the

The construction of information system serves for social assistance.

Ministry of Civil Affairs, the Ministry of Human Resources and Social Security and other ministries released the *Opinions on Further Improving the Urban and Rural Medical Relief System, Opinions on Pilot Programs of Medical Aid for Major and Serious Diseases*, and *Opinions on Integrating the New Rural and Urban Resident Pension Insurance System with the Urban Resident Minimum Subsistence Allowance and Five-Guarantee Household Support System* to further improve the urban-rural medical relief system and enable it to link with the new medical care system reform and the urban-rural subsistence allowance system. Meanwhile, the central government, on the basis of enlarging the coverage of the urban-rural minimum subsistence allowance system and setting up the medical relief system, has set up and further improved disaster relief, temporary relief, Five-Guarantee households support, rural poverty-stricken household relief and beggar relief system, and made obvious achievements in social charity, social donation and mutual assistance and other social support programs and volunteer service system building.

Statistics show that by the end of 2012, China had 11.149 million households under the urban minimum subsistence allowance system, totaling 21.435 million beneficiaries. And the fiscal expenditures at all levels reached RMB 67.43 billion. Rural areas had 28.149 million households under the minimum subsistence allowance system, or 53.445 million beneficiaries, and the fiscal expenditures at all levels reached 71.8 billion yuan. The Five-Guarantee households in the rural area totaled 5.292 million households, with 5.456 million beneficiaries. A total of 796,000 persons were supported by the traditional relief in rural areas and 99,000 urban residents who had no source of income, no capacity of labor and no legal supporter received aid. The medical relief system offered help to 20.77 million urban residents and 59.742 million poverty-stricken farmers, and issued medical aid to 4.045 million of beneficiaries. A total of 6.398 million of people enjoyed temporary relief in the whole year. In addition, progress was made in education relief, housing relief and juridical relief, enriching the social relief services and benefiting more needy people. A social relief system,

An ill worker received the relief funds from China Soong Ching Ling Foundation.

with the urban-rural minimum subsistence allowance, Five-Guarantee system of rural areas, disaster relief, and medical relief as the foundation was set up. The system is consistent to the low-rent housing, education, juridical relief and other special relief systems, setting up the final guarantee measure for needy people.

In February 2014, China issued the first administrative regulations – *Interim Measures on Social Relief* to coordinate the social relief systems, stipulating the minimum subsistence allowance, support for needy people, disaster victim relief, medical relief, education relief, housing relief, employment relief and temporary relief and participation of the social forces as the basic content, in order to define a complete social relief system. The measures offer help to those in emergency and difficulty in a sustainable way, consistent with other social security systems and the social and economic development level.

Social Welfare

With deepening state-owned enterprise reform, the number of state-owned enterprises and their employees both decreased. What's more, the welfare services for employees of the state-owned enterprises, organs and institutional units were socialized gradually. Consequently input in welfare services decreased significantly and so did burdens. Meanwhile, although not meeting the requirements of the masses, the traditional social welfare services developed noticeably, with improved social welfare facilities in urban and rural areas and enhanced functions. The elderly, children (orphans, the disabled, street children) and the disabled were given priority. According to statistics from the Ministry of Civil Affairs, China has 48,000 social service agencies providing accommodation (11,000 registered as the institutional units), totaling 4.493 million of beds, or 3.3 beds per 1,000 people; and accepted 3.095 million persons. Of that, 44,304 were pension service agencies with 4.165 million beds, or 21.5 beds per 1,000 elderly,

Table 4-2-1
Social Relief Since 2005
Unit: 10,000 People

Index	2005	2006	2007	2008	2009	2010	2011	2012
Number of urban minimum subsistence allowance beneficiaries	2234.2	2240.1	2272.1	2334.8	2345.6	2310.5	2276.8	2143.5
Number of rural minimum subsistence allowance beneficiaries	825.0	1593.1	3566.3	4305.5	4760.0	5214.0	5305.7	5344.5
Number of beneficiaries under the rural Five-Guarantee Household system	300	503.3	531.3	548.6	553.4	556.3	551	545.6

Data source: *2012 Statistical Bulletin of Social Service Development*, Ministry of Civil Affairs.

and accepted 2.936 million elderly by the end of the year. In addition, China also had set up service agencies for the mentally retarded and mental patients, children welfare, children relief and relief workstations and other social service agencies that provided accommodation. The social services that do not provide accommodation include elderly services, child welfare, welfare enterprises, social relief, disaster prevention and relief, charities, veteran benefits and relocation, community services, etc. By the end of 2012, China had set up 200,000 community service providers, covering 29.5% of communities. The coverage of urban community service centers (stations) was 72.5%. China also had 397,000 service stations for the public and 93,000 community volunteer organizations.

However, China also saw contributions of social welfare services from the social organizations, mass self-government organizations and all walks of society. In 2012, the State Council promulgated *Several Opinions of the State Council on Encouraging and Guiding the Healthy Development of Private Investment*, encouraging private investment to participate in social welfare

The orphans in Taihu County, Anhui Province received educational grants.

services and set up various social welfare service organizations by means of offering land guarantees, credit support, government procurement and other means. The Ministry of Civil Affairs released the *Opinions on Supporting Social Forces to Set up Social Welfare Organizations*. In terms of the welfare guarantee, an elderly social welfare service system was set up with elderly social welfare organizations as the backbone, community elderly welfare services as the basis, and home care as the foundation, improving the social security network to protect the basic living rights and interests of the needy elderly. The amended *Law of the People's Republic of China on Protection of Minors* clearly stipulated that minors have the right to live, to develop, and to be protected, the right of participation and the right to education, highlighting the principle of the priority of minors, and reinforced responsibilities of the government, society, schools and families to frame a "blue sky" for the healthy growth of minors. In 2010 and 2011, the General Office of the State Council promulgated the *Opinions on Enforcing Orphan Protection* and the *Opinions on Enforcing and Improving the Relief and Protection to Vagrant Minors* to further improve the protection and relief system of orphans and vagrant minors. A legal system has been set up with the constitution as the basis; the criminal, civil and administrative laws as the foundation; the law on protection of the disabled as the center; and regulations on

Table 4-2-2
2005-2012 Beds in Social Service Institutions
Unit: 10,000 Beds

Index	2005	2006	2007	2008	2009	2010	2011	2012
Number of beds	180.7	204.5	269.6	300.3	326.5	349.6	396.4	449.3
Beds per 1000 persons	1.38	1.56	2.04	2.26	2.45	2.61	2.61	3.32

Data source: 2012 Statistical Bulletin of Social Service Development, Ministry of Civil Affairs.

education and employment of the disabled and local provisions that benefit and support the disabled as complementary instruments. The system, involving more than 50 laws, aims to protect rights and interests of the disabled in an all-round way and promote development of the undertakings related to the disabled. In addition, compulsory education was made free of charge and the high school and higher education systems started to offer aid to the poverty-stricken students.

Scope and Service System of Social Security

Entering the 12th Five-Year Plan period (2011–2015), China has expanded the social security system from urban areas to rural areas, from state-owned enterprises to all kinds of employers, from the workers to the people with flexible employment and urban and rural residents. More and more people enjoy basic social security services, many historical problems have been addressed, and the social security level has been improved. The social security management system has taken shape with establishment of a service network, with the social

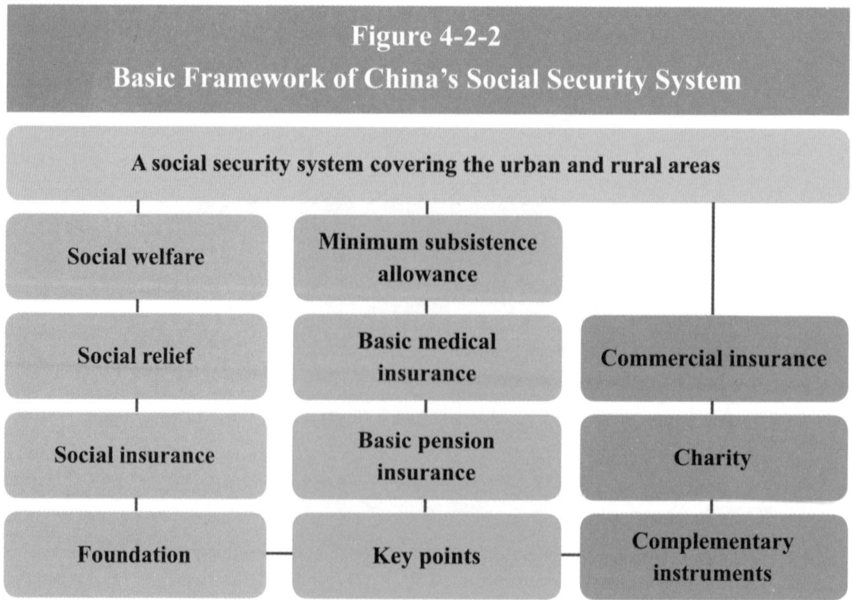

insurance agencies at all levels as the backbone, banks and other designated service providers as support, and the community labor guarantee platform as the foundation. The system was gradually expanded to the townships, towns and administrative villages. The Golden Insurance Project (a unified labor and social security e-governance project of China) Phase I was completed successfully with the three-tier (central, provincial and municipal tiers) networks interlinked. By the end of January 2014, China has issued 560 million of unified social security cards and the number is expected to reach 660 million by the end of the year and 800 million in 2015, covering 60% of the total population of China, offering technical support for the overall arrangement and integration of the urban and rural social security systems. By the end of 2012, the balance of the social security funds was RMB 491.5 billion, the balance of accumulated deposits reached RMB 4.0943 trillion. The funds are complete and safe.

Establishment and Improvement of the Housing Guarantee System

Housing Commercialization and the "Affordable Housing Project"

Traditionally China's urban housing system was characterized by national turnkey allocation: free of charge, low rent, and use without limit on duration. On the eve of reform and opening up, the defects of the system had been fully exposed (too much debt, a heavy burden, unfair allocation and distorted consumption structure). More importantly, the supply of housing was short and the system was unsustainable. Considering the situation, Deng Xiaoping

The housing security system has been established in China for 20 years.

talked about housing system reform in 1978 and 1980, respectively. China started to promote housing commercialization and socialization from 1994, correspondingly the housing accumulation fund system was established.

In July 1994, the State Council promulgated the *Decision on Deepening Urban Housing System Reform*, and put forward to set up a low-cost housing system for families with middle and low incomes and a commercial housing supply system for high-income families. The provision could be considered a symbol of the launch of the urban resident housing guarantee system that was adapted to the socialist market economy. On July 3, 1998, the *Circular of the State Council on Further Enforcing the Urban Housing System Reform and Accelerating the Housing Construction* was promulgated, which put forward three important sets of goals: (1) to stop housing allocation, monetize housing distribution, adjust the housing investment structure with priority given to low-

By the end of 2013, 34 million housing problems has been solved for urban families in total.

income housing development and accelerating housing problem solution for needy urban residents; (2) to set up and improve a low-income-housing-based housing supply system, exercise different housing supply policies for households with different incomes; the lowest-income families could rent the low-cost housing supplied by the government or employers, the low and middle income families could purchase low-cost housing; high-income families could purchase or rent commercial housing with market-regulated prices; (3) to grant housing subsidies. Afterward a new housing guarantee system consistent with the new housing system made its first appearance.

The large-scale low-income housing construction started in 1995 was called the "Affordable Housing Project". In the early days of 1995, the Housing System Reform Leading Group of the State Council promulgated the *Implementation Plan of the State Affordable Housing Project*, moving to add 150 million square meters of low-income housing on the basis of the existing housing construction plan over five years, beginning in1995. The low-income housing would be sold to the middle- and low-income families at cost and priority would be given to the families without a house, or living in the dilapidated buildings or having housing problems and the retirees or teachers with housing problems under the same conditions. Low-income housing could not be sold to high-income families. In 1998 when substantial steps were taken in housing monetization, the construction of low-cost housing was enforced in various areas. In 1999, the Ministry of Housing and Urban-Rural Development and the relevant departments formulated the *Measures for Administration of Urban Low-Rent Housing, the Measures for Administration of Application, Review and Quit of Low-rent Housing of Lowest-income Families, Interim Measures for Sale of Purchased Public Housing and Low-cost Housing*, and other regulations and rules to make institutional preparations for the new housing guarantee system.

However, entering in the new century, especially since 2003 when the *Circular of the State Council on Promoting the Continuous and Healthy Development of the Real Estate Markets* was promulgated, various areas,

The hot property market begins to cool down in China.

observing the concept of urban management and housing marketization, tried to build the real estate sector as the pillar sector, sell land and vigorously develop the commercial housing, resulting in rising price of the real estate. The investment in the low-income housing was not prioritized, and the distribution was seriously unfair. What's more, the objectives of low-rent housing system were not realized and the basic housing requirement of the masses could not be met, causing many social conflicts. To address the problems, the General Office of the State Council released the *Circular on Earnestly Stabilizing the Real Estate Price* on March 26, 2005, and took various measures to regulate the overheating real estate market and check the rising trend of the real estate prices. However, the demand management did not change with the supply structure, and the Affordable Housing Project was implemented slowly. The situation was noticeably changed only after the State Council promulgated the *Several*

Opinions on Solving the Housing Difficulties of the Low-income Families in 2007, and thereafter with the outbreak of the international financial crisis in 2008.

Gradual Improvement of the Low-income Housing System and Noticeably Enforced Construction Intensity

After several years of efforts in real estate market regulation, the Chinese government has enforced the building and improvement of the housing guarantee system, and gradually clarified the responsibilities of the government and main purpose of macro regulation: to strengthen the government's housing guarantee functions, accelerate the construction of low-rent housing system for urban residents, standardize the development of low-cost housing, actively develop the secondary housing market and the rental market and solve the housing difficulties of low-income families step by step. In 2007, the promulgation of the *Several Opinions of the State Council on Solving the Housing Difficulties of Urban Low-income Families* indicated the return to the right direction from overemphasis on market to equal emphasis on both the market and the guarantee system and from the "emphasis on house purchasing and downplaying renting" to "equal emphasis on renting and sales of housing".

The largest highlight of real estate market reform in 2007 was the further clarification of the objective and basic framework of the housing guarantee system, i.e. further improving the urban low-rent housing system for low-income urban families, improving and standardizing the low-income housing system and enforcing renovation of shanty towns and dilapidated residential areas to significantly improve the living conditions of the low-income families. The same year, the 17th National Congress of the CPC moved to achieve the objective of "everyone having access to housing". For this purpose, the government started to accelerate construction of low-income housing. In March 2009, the Chinese government accelerated implementation and improvement of low-income housing construction policies and measures to address the housing problems of 7.5

Many people has lived a happy life with the help of the Housing Project for Low-income Families by government.

million of urban low-income families and 2.4 million households of residents in forest areas, reclamation areas and coal mining shanty towns within three years. Of the important public investment programs within the budget of the central government in 2009, RMB 49.3 billion was invested in construction of low-rent housing, renovation of shanty towns, pilot projects of rural dilapidated building renovation and settlement of nomadic ethnic groups. The relevant departments of the State Council formulated the low-rent housing guarantee plan, promulgated instructive opinions on the renovation of dilapidated rural buildings and decided to offer housing for rent and rent subsidies to address the housing problems of 2.6 million low-income urban families. The government added 1.77 million low-rent suites, granted rent subsidies to 830,000 households, solved the housing renovation of 800,000 families in the forest areas, reclamation areas and coal mining areas, helped 800,000 poverty-stricken families renovate the dilapidated rural buildings and continued efforts in promoting settlement of nomads. In 2010 the State Council released the *Circular on Resolutely Curbing the Soaring Housing Prices in Some Cities*, and required accelerated construction of low-income housing. The land for low-income housing, shanty town renovation, and small- and medium-sized common commercial housing shall not be lower than 70% of the total land supply for housing construction, and such projects would be given priority in the land supply. In areas with soaring housing prices, the supply of public rental housing, low-cost housing and price-capped housing would be significantly increased. The objective of building 3 million units of low-income housing and renovating 2.8 million units of shanty town homes in 2010 was also declared.

In the same year, the Ministry of Housing and Urban-Rural Development and six other ministries jointly formulated the *Guiding Opinions on Accelerating the Development of Public Rental Housing*. The central economic work conference convened at the end of the year recommended to "accelerate construction of the housing guarantee system, enforce construction of low-income housing, and gradually form a low-income housing system and commercial housing system that conforms to China's actual situation". In 2011, the Chinese government declared that in the 12th Five-Year Plan period, the urban low-income housing coverage shall reach about 20%; 10 million units of low-income housing and renovated housing in shanty towns would be constructed in 2011; and real estate market regulation policies would be further carried out and improved to resolutely curb the soaring real estate prices in some cities. In the same year, the central government had made great efforts to implement and improve real estate market regulation policies, increase the scale of low-income housing and set up the assessment and accountability system. In 2012, China launched construction of 7.7 million units of low-income housing construction

Figure 4-3-1
Basic Framework of China's Housing Guarantee System

Affordable Housing Project

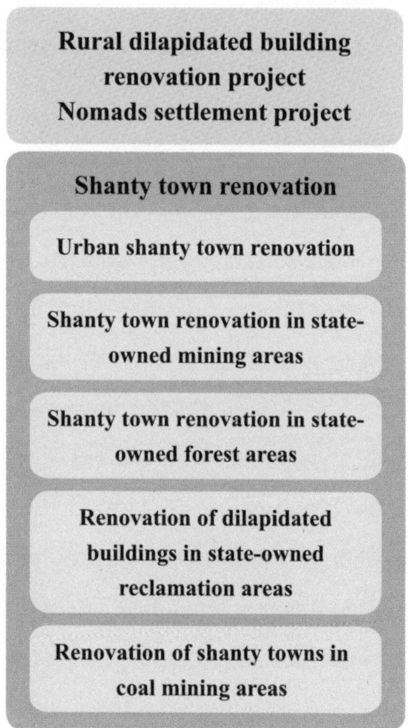

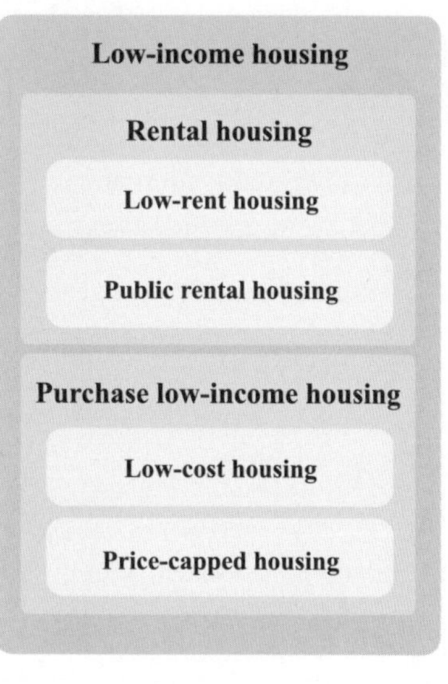

Figure 4-3-2
Growth of Beneficiaries of the Urban Housing Guarantee System

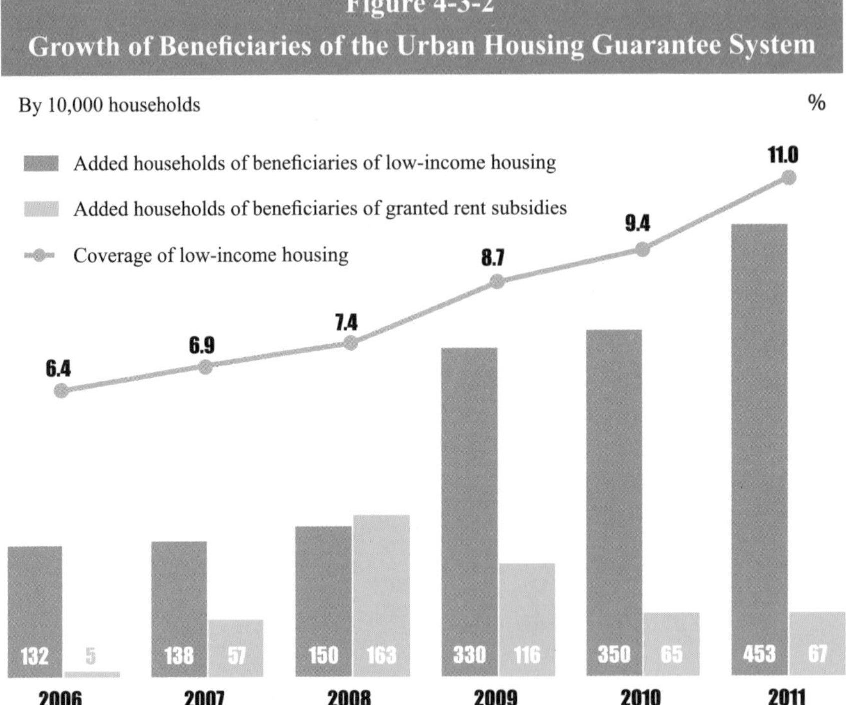

and shanty town renovation and 5.5 million sets were completed, exceeding the stated objective from the beginning of the year. In 2013 low-income housing was constructed on a large scale and the objectives were to complete construction of 4.6 million units, begin construction of 6 million sets and complete renovation of 3 million dilapidated rural homes. According to primary statistics, China solved the housing problems of 26.5 million low- and lower-middle-income urban households, accounting for 11% of all urban households. This statistic includes beneficiaries of low-rent housing, low-cost housing, price-capped housing, public rental housing, and beneficiaries of shanty town renovation programs. In addition, nearly 4.5 million households enjoyed housing subsidies. In total more than 30 million households benefited from the housing guarantee system, or nearly 100 million people, if assuming the average household has three members.

The new modern residential houses have been built after the reconstruction of shanty towns in the forest of Greater Khingan Mountains.

Generally speaking, the five years from 2008 to 2012 witnessed the largest-scale construction and highest input in low-income housing in China's, with construction starting on more than 30 million units of urban low-income housing and completion of 17 million units, solving the housing problems of the low- and middle-income families in the urban area. Meanwhile, the dilapidated rural building renovation program was implemented nationwide with 10.334 million poverty-stricken families receiving assistance. From 2014, the low-rent housing system and the public rental housing system were integrated and public rental housing and shanty town renovation are expected to become the focus of the low-income housing construction. The low-cost housing and price-capped housing that was supplied with ownership would die out. At the same time, the development of shared-ownership housing would be encouraged to mobilize the masses' enthusiasm to improve living conditions.

However, so far the housing guarantee system is mainly for the urban residents, including the floating population. The rural area is not yet involved.

Since the 17th National Congress of the CPC, efforts have been increased regarding shoddy and dilapidated building renovation for needy farmers. Low-cost housing and incentivized housing have been built. Minhou of Fujian Province also attempted to set up a rural housing guarantee system combining housing supply and rental subsidies. In April 2011, Chengdu, which carried out pilot projects of an urban-rural coordination program, declared it would set up a rural housing guarantee system by 2012 and promulgated the *Implementation Opinions on Establishment of the Rural Housing Guarantee System* (trial). This was called the first rural housing guarantee system of China by the media and the most thorough detailed regulations for the household registration system reform in Chengdu.

Main Issues and Prospects in the 12th Five-Year Plan Period

Main Issues

Since the reform and opening up policy was implemented in China, the social security undertaking of China experienced two stages, one before and one after the 16th National Congress of the CPC in 2002. The first stage witnessed reconstruction and formation of the social insurance-based social security system and the latter stage saw urban-rural coordination-centered innovation and development of the social security system (the housing guarantee was in the first stage). In recent years, China made achievements in the social security development in the following four areas: formation of a system and framework and institutional transformation; enlarging coverage and steadily increasing treatment; addressing many historical problems related to the institutional transition, offering strong support for state-owned enterprise reform and economic structure adjustment; promoting a socialized management service system to take shape and reducing burdens of the enterprises and institutional units regarding the social affairs. Practice has shown that social security is an important guarantee for social stability and order and an important foundation for the stability of the state, the people's happiness, and sustained economic growth. Establishing and improving the social security system is an important part of the socialist market economic system, and is related to the immediate interests of the masses, continuity of reform and opening up, modernization and the long-term stability of China, and of great significance to regulating the income distribution, improving social justice, enlarging domestic demand and driving economic growth.

南方日報 号外

南方日报社出版 责编：青仙 版式：小波

高度决定影响力

2002年11月8日 星期五

党的十六大上午开幕 江泽民作报告提出

全面建设小康社会

■江泽民在报告中说，本次大会的主题是：高举邓小平理论伟大旗帜，全面贯彻"三个代表"重要思想，继往开来，与时俱进，全面建设小康社会，加快推进社会主义现代化，为开创中国特色社会主义事业新局面而奋斗

■江泽民在报告中总结了党领导人民建设中国特色社会主义必须坚持的"十条基本经验"，提出全面建设小康社会的奋斗目标：我们要在本世纪头二十年，集中力量，全面建设惠及十几亿人口的更高水平的小康社会，使经济更加发展、民主更加健全、科教更加进步、文化更加繁荣、社会更加和谐、人民生活更加殷实；经过这个阶段的建设，再继续奋斗几十年，到本世纪中叶基本实现现代化，把我国建成富强民主文明的社会主义国家

江泽民向大会作报告

十六大举世瞩目 新华社发

大会为已故老一辈革命家默哀

江泽民作报告体现改革精神

Inaugurated on Nov. 8th, 2002, the 16th National Congress of Communist Party of China proposed to build a moderately prosperous society in all aspects.

China enjoys various advantages in the next step of development of the social security. The government has attached great importance to construction of the social security system and offered a solid political foundation for accelerating development of the system. In more than 30 years of rcform and opening up, China has made remarkable achievements in economic development and greatly enhanced its comprehensive strength, offering a strong economic foundation for accelerating construction of the social security system. Social development has come to a new stage, and the people's living standards have been obviously improved. The people have strengthened their awareness of social security and increased expectations of social security, laying a good social foundation for accelerating development of the system. With more than 20 years of reform and exploration, China has accumulated valuable experiences and laid a solid practical base for accelerating development of the social security system.

While fully aware of the advantages of accelerating development of the social security system, we must soberly concede that China's social security system is not complete, the social security systems in the urban and the rural areas are not balanced, with seriously lagging social security in rural areas The coverage of some basic guarantee systems is narrow. With ongoing urbanization, the requirements are becoming increasingly urgent and difficulties are increasing with regard to enforcing system integration and unifying management services. Gaps in the social security benefits between urban and rural residents and other groups are large and the contradiction is obvious. The population is aging faster and most of the individual accounts of the pension insurance system are empty, adding increasing pressure to the long-term fund balance, value maintenance and appreciation. Problems such as low coordination level of social insurance, unbalanced development of informatization and an incomplete management service system have not been fully solved, thereby hampering development of the social security system and basic public service equalization. The unbalanced development of the components and elements of the social security system and the difficulties of getting medical care and high expenses of medical care for the common people have not been fully alleviated and there is still the arduous task of solving the housing difficulties of the needy.

Case Study: Pension System

Let's analyze and explain the "fragmentation" of the pension system that has been much criticized. Generally it is considered that China exercises a dual-track system for the old-age security, i.e. a system for the organs and institutional units and a system for the enterprise employees, with the latter receiving a much lower pension than the former, even lower than the pension replacement rate alert line18. In fact, China's pension system is not a dual-track system, but a multi-track one. Zheng Bingwen, director of the World Social Security Research Center of Chinese Academy of Social Sciences, said, "At present system fragmentation is very serious. For example, Shanghai has four social security

News cartoon: The Minimum Living Allowance as the Last Defense for Low-income Families.

People are confused about the "fragmentation" of the pension security system in China.

systems: urban social security, town social security, rural social security and comprehensive social security. If including the institutional units and the public servant systems, Shanghai has six systems. The problem is that the gaps among these systems are large and the systems run independently of each other, resulting in an unreasonable situation. The systems short of funds need transfer payment while the systems rich in funds leave funds to depreciate for years. The situation of Shanghai is a microcosm of China, fully reflecting the serious institutional defects.... The situation must be addressed by setting up a unified social security system."

However, it is not easy to set up a unified social security system across the country. It is widely agreed that integration of these systems is imperative and the principle of integration should be justice and sustainability. But how to integrate? And which standard should be followed in the process? The integration must involve interest adjustment and redistribution of resources, affecting the whole country. So it is very difficult. Let's take the integration of the old-age security systems for government organs and institutional units and enterprises as an example. In February 2008, the State Council promulgated the *Pilot Program for Reform of the Institutional Unit Pension Insurance System* and decided to introduce pilot programs for reform of the institutional unit pension insurance systems in Shanxi, Shanghai, Zhejiang, Guangdong and Chongqing. However, the reform was tardy, although five years have passed. It is because the reform touches the immediate interests of the staff members of the institutional units which are waiting to see how the public servant system is reformed. Here is another example: the placement rate of the urban basic pension insurance has declined to a very low level and it cannot sustain if adhering to the retirement age stipulated by the existing system. However, the proposal of raising the retirement age has been fiercely opposed. The latest research indicates that if the existing pension system is executed continuously and the retirement age and other standards are not adjusted, the national employee pension insurance system would be beyond its means and need to use the accumulated balance by 2023. By 2050, the fiscal subsidies would be increased to 8.46% of the GDP to maintain proper operation of the pension system, or 34.85% of the fiscal expenditures of the year, i.e. about one third of the fiscal expenditures would be used for making up the gap of the pension insurance. Obviously, it is much more difficult to reform distribution of the "cake" than to enlarge it. Anyway as long as the common understanding of reform is reached, the greatest common divisor will be found. It is unquestionable for the CPC and the Chinese government to tackle the difficulties. The new measure of establishing a unified urban-rural basic pension insurance system is a good start.

Plan for Deepening the Reform

Facing the new requirements and new challenges in this new stage, the 17th National Congress of the CPC made arrangements on how to develop the social security undertaking in a faster and better way. The *Twelfth Five-Year Plan for National Economic and Social Development of China* sticks to the

Figure 4-4-1 Scope and Key Areas of Basic Public Services During the 12th Five-Year Plan Period	
1	**Public education**
	(1). nine-year compulsory education free of charge; accommodation fees exempted in boarding schools in rural areas during the years of compulsory education;
	(2). secondary vocational education free of charge for rural students, students from urban families in economic difficulties and students studying agriculture-related majors;
	(3). subsidies provided to children from families in economic difficulties, orphaned and disabled children to receive pre-school education.
2	**Employment service**
	(1). provide employment info, consultation, referral, labor mediation and arbitration services to urban and rural laborers free of charge;
	(2). provide basic vocational training free of charge to unemployed people, rural migrant workers, the disabled people, and new laborers;
	(3). provide employment assistance to people with employment difficulties and zero-employment families.
3	**Social security**
	(1). urban employees and residents to enjoy basic pension scheme, and rural residents to enjoy new countryside social pension scheme;
	(2). urban employees and residents to enjoy basic medical insurance, and rural residents to enjoy new countryside cooperative medical scheme;
	(3). urban employees to enjoy unemployment insurance, work injury insurance and maternity insurance;
	(4). provide urban and rural residents living in economic difficulties with minimum living allowances, medical assistance, funeral and internet assistance and other services;
	(5). provide welfare services to special groups of people including orphaned children, disabled people, households enjoying the five guarantees (childless and infirm old persons who are guaranteed food, clothing, medical care, housing and burial expenses), and elderly seniors.

4	**Medical and health service** (1). Provide free health records, preventive vaccination, infectious disease control, child health, maternal health care, elder care, health education, hypertension and other chronic disease management, management of severe mental illness, and other basic public health services; (2). implement important public health services such as prevention and control of AIDS, tuberculosis, folic acid supplements for rural women before pregnancy and during early pregnancy, hospital maternity benefits for rural women, cervical cancer and breast cancer checks of rural women, cataract-extraction surgery of the poverty- stricken groups; (3). implement the national essential drug system, and essential drugs are included in the basic Medicare drug reimbursement list.
5	**Population and family planning** (1). Provide free contraceptives, pre-pregnancy examination, reproductive health technologies, publicity and other family planning services; (2). offer re-production technical services for those of childbearing age.
6	**Housing security** (1). provide low-rent housing to urban low-income families with housing difficulties; (2). provide public rental housing to urban lower-middle-income families with housing difficulties.
7	**Public culture** (1). Free grassroots public cultural and sports facilities; (2). full coverage of radio and TV of the rural area; offer free film, books, newspaper and opera delivery and other public cultural services for the rural area.
8	**Infrastructure** (1). Enable all administrative villages to have highways and bus services , full coverage of the public transportation services to urban areas; (2). enable electricity supply to all the administrative villages and the population of the areas that had no electricity supply in the past; (3). postal services in every township and villages.
9	**Environmental protection** (1). Every county will have the capability of sewage and waste harmless treatment and environmental monitoring and assessment; (2). The urban and rural drinking water sources are protected.

principle of prioritizing the people's livelihood and makes overall arrangements for income distribution, social security, public service system construction, medical care, education and housing. The 12th Five-Year Plan period is a critical period for China to build a well-off society, overcome obstacles in accelerating the transformation of the economic development modes and promote steady and fast economic development. It is also an important period for deepening reform in social security and making breakthroughs in critical junctures. According to the spirit of the 17th National Congress of the CPC and the 12th Five-Year Plan, the main goals of China in social security development by 2015 are as follows: a sound social security system will be basically completed, with enlarged coverage, steadily improved guarantee levels, and historical problems basically solved, a moderate, sustainable and stable social security network for building a well-off society in an all-round way will be provided. In terms of the system building, efforts will be made to build complete security systems. The reform of the pension insurance system of organs and institutional units is steadily promoted and the existing security systems are improved. Progress will be made in urban-rural coordination and the multi-level guarantee system shall be further improved. In terms of coverage, efforts will be made to cover all the population with a basic pension insurance system and basic medical insurance system. The participants of basic urban pension insurance will reach 357 million, including 307 million participants in the enterprise basic pension insurance system. Participants of the new rural cooperative insurance system will reach 450 million. The participation rate of the urban-rural basic medical insurance system will increased by 3 percentage points according to the baseline of 2010 data. The participants of the work-related injury insurance will reach 210 million, unemployment insurance will reach 160 million and maternity insurance will reach 150 million. The minimum subsistence allowance will be granted to all those covered by the system. As for the guarantee levels, efforts will be made to continuously improve social insurance benefit standards and enable stable growth of the basic pension of enterprise employees, urban resident social pension insurance and new rural social pension insurance. The public payment of hospitalization expenses of workers' basic medical insurance, urban residents' basic medical insurance and the new rural social medical insurance will account for 70% of the total. The pooling for outpatient services of the urban resident basic medical insurance and the new rural social medical insurance will cover all the pooling areas and the pooling for workers' outpatient services by basic medical insurance will be promoted steadily. We will consistently improve treatment standards for unemployment insurance, work-related injury insurance and maternity insurance as well as the urban and rural minimum subsistence allowances, and enable employees with disability caused by work-related injuries to enjoy basic vocational rehabilitation services. In terms of building the service system, we will work hard to form an employment and social security public service network for all of society, and urge sub-districts (communities), townships and towns (administrative villages) to complete primary employment and social security service platforms. Administrative villages will implement the employment and social security coordination system. Fully functional basic social security service facilities with a reasonable structure and information networking shall be set up at the county level and above. The holders of the national unified social security card will reach 800 million. The proportion of enterprise retirees covered by the community management system will reach 80%. The social pension service system and the child welfare service system will be improved. The disabled service system and the migrant workers' family care service system will be established. The frequent social donation system will be further improved with frequent donation stations and charity supermarkets set up in towns and townships (sub-districts).

In November 2013, the third plenary session of the 18th National Congress of the CPC released the *Decision on Some Major Issues Concerning Comprehensively Deepening the Reform*, and announced several goals for social security system reform: (1) Instituting a fairer and more sustainable social security system. We will adhere to the basic pension system that combines

Figure 4-4-2 Action Plan to Improve People's Livelihood	
1	**Expand urban and rural employment** Create 9 million new jobs on average each year in urban areas; urbanize 8 million rural laborers annually. The rate of signing labor contracts by enterprises to reach 90%; the rate of signing collective employment contracts to reach 80%.
2	**Increase the minimum wage standard** Minimum wage to increase by no less than 13% on average each year. The minimum wage in vast majority of areas to be no less than 40% of the average wage of the local urban employees.
3	**Improve the pension scheme standard** Achieve nationwide coordination of a basic pension fund for urban employees. Increase the number of urban residents newly enrolled in the pension insurance scheme by 100 million people. Steadily increase the basic pension received by urban employees; urban non-employed residents above the age of 60 to enjoy basic pension. Achieve full coverage of new countryside social pension scheme, and increase the standard of basic pension.
4	**Improve the standard of medical insurance** Increase the number of urban and rural residents newly enrolled in the basic medical insurance scheme by 60 million people. Steadily increase the level of subsidies from fiscal budget to the basic medical insurance scheme and the new countryside cooperative medical scheme; the percentage of payment covered by the medical insurance fund within policy scope to increase to over 70%.
5	**Increase the urban and rural minimum living standards** Increase the minimum living standards for urban and rural residents by over 10% on average each year.
6	**Reduce the number of rural residents living in poverty** Increase inputs for poverty alleviation; steadily increase the standard of poverty alleviation; and substantially reduce the number of people living in poverty
7	**Cut taxes for residents** Increase the personal income and wage tax deduction threshold, and reasonably adjust the tax rate structure for personal income tax in the early phase of the 12th Five-Year period; establish and improve the personal income tax system with a combination of integration and classification in the middle and late phase of the 12th Five-Year period.

8	**Implement housing projects for low-income urban residents** Construct and renovate 36 million apartments for urban low-income families; the coverage of low-income housing will reach 20% nationwide. No less than 10% of the net income from land assignment to be used for construction of low-income housing and renovation of units in run-down areas.
9	**Improve the employment and social security service system** Reinforce the building of service facilities for public employment, social security, labor inspection, mediation and arbitration services. Promote the use of social security all-in-one card. The number of standard social security insurance cards issued nationwide to reach 800 million, covering 60% of the population.
10	**Increase the proportion of state-owned assets gains spent on people's livelihood** Enlarge the scope of state-owned assets gains that should be handed in to the state; steadily increase the percentage collected from the state-owned assets gains, with the incremental part mainly used for expenditures on people's livelihood such as social security.

social pools with individual accounts, improve the individual accounts system, complete the incentive mechanism in which those who contribute more will get more, guarantee the rights and interests of the insured, place basic pensions under unified national planning, and uphold the principle of balance based on actuarial mathematics. We will push forward the reform of the pension system for government organs and public institutions. We will integrate the basic pension and medical care insurance systems for urban and rural residents and expedite the balanced development of the minimum living allowance system in both urban and rural areas. We will establish and improve a social security benefits calculation and regular adjustment mechanism that gives appropriate consideration to various groups. We will improve policies on the transfer and continuation of social insurance, extend insurance coverage to more groups of people, and reduce the social insurance premiums appropriately and in a timely manner. We will study and work out a policy to progressively raise the retirement age. We will speed up the improvement of a social security management system and service network. We will improve a housing security and supply system consistent with our national conditions, create an open and standard housing provident fund system, and improve the regulations on the withdrawal, use and supervision of the provident fund. (2) We will improve a financial input system for the budgeting system of social security. We will strengthen management of and supervision over investment of social insurance funds, and encourage funds to be invested into diversified sectors in the market. We will enact preferential policies, such as tax exemption and deferral, and encourage the development of enterprise annuity, occupational annuity and commercial insurance, so as to bring into shape a multi-level social security system. (3) We will respond actively to the aging of the population, quicken steps in the establishment of a social endowment service system and development of the service industry for the elderly. We will improve the caring service system for children, women and seniors left behind in the rural areas and a classified security system to protect the rights and interests of the disabled and children in difficulties. (4) We will steadily promote the basic

An appropriate public service system with social welfare for all citizens has been established in China.

public services to enable full coverage of the permanent population, include farmers who relocate to urban areas and integrate pension and medical insurance regulations with the urban social security system.

Although the special planning on the housing guarantee has not been promulgated, the objectives have been clarified: we will give priority to solving the housing problem of low-income families. In this period, efforts shall be made to increase the supply of low-rent housing and low-cost housing by means of renovation of shanty towns, construction of new housing, government procurement and rent and increasing housing rental subsidies to solve the housing problems of low-income families in urban areas. After basically solving the housing problems of 15.40 million households by the end of 2012, we will steadily enlarge institutional coverage, appropriately increase guarantee standards and try to ensure housing of low-income families with the per capita living area below 13 square meters according to actual situations of various areas from 2013 to 2015. For lower-middle income families, the supply of public rental housing, low-cost housing and price-capped housing will be increased. There are also requirements on the schedule of the renovation programs of shanty towns and dilapidated buildings. Meanwhile, efforts shall be made to accelerate legislation of housing guarantees, enforce responsibilities of the government at all levels regarding the housing guarantee, improve the support system of organizations, policies and technologies, implement research on key technologies for housing guarantee and application demonstration and accelerate informatization. By the end of 2012, all counties and cities shall improve the housing guarantee administrative bodies and specific implementation bodies and realize inter-linkage of the housing guarantee business systems nationwide. By the end of 2015, the national housing guarantee information management platform will be completed. The *Decision on Some Major Issues Concerning Comprehensively Deepening the Reform* described the housing guarantee simply, "We will improve a housing security and supply system consistent with our national conditions, create an open and standard housing provident fund system, and improve the regulations on the withdrawal, use and supervision of the provident fund." On September 25, 2013, the State Council made the following decisions at the executive meeting: (1) To properly increase the subsidy funds, focus on support of construction of low-income housing programs, especially construction of the supporting facilities for completed low-income housing; study multi-channel funds to support construction of the low-income housing; those areas where low-income housing is idle shall take active measures to eliminate such a situation. (2) To accelerate formulation of urban housing guarantee regulations, standardize and promote construction, management and operation of low-income housing to stabilize the people's expectations of "access to housing". (3) To speed up integration of public rental housing and low-rent housing systems. Efforts shall be made to design and improve transparent public rental housing allocation policies and make good use of the rent lever and enforce access and quit management. Differential subsidies will be granted according to the incomes of needy families.

Based on the abovementioned general planning and special planning, it can be predicted that in the coming five years, China's social security system building will stride toward the general inclusive goals put forward at the 17th National Congress of the CPC to ensure that all our people enjoy their rights to education, employment, medical and old-age care and housing. Through the *12th Five-Year Plan for National System of Basic Public Service* - the first state-level plan that involves basic public services, put forward that in the 12th Five-Year Plan period, we will further innovate through a new system and new mechanism, enforce the capacity of public services delivery, accelerate building of a basic public service system that is sustainable and consistent with the actual situation of China, try to improve the level of public services and equalization, promote coordinated economic and social development and lay a solid foundation for building a well-off society. The social security system is a mechanism for a state to mitigate the risks of civil society. It consists of social security institutional arrangement and service systems. Of that, the social security service system is an important part of the public service system. A sound public service system can offer a good service platform and assistance for development. Of course, China shall pay attention to learning experiences and lessons from Western countries and make decisions according to the actual situation to avoid the welfare dependency and excessive welfare. What China has focused on is a moderately inclusive public service system that can meet the requirements of building a moderately prosperous society in an all-round way, including the social security system. Here "moderate" is a very important requirement.

Notes

18. The pension replacement rate is the percentage of the pension in the salary. The data indicates that the basic pension insurance replacement rare decreased from 72.9% in 2002 to 57.7% in 2005 and kept the decline trend to 50.3% in 2011. The World Bank suggests that to maintain the living standards before retirement, the pension replacement rate shall not be lower than 70%; the International Labor Organization suggests that the pension replacement rate shall not be lower than 55% the lowest. Please refer to China's Enterprise Pension Replacement rate Falls below the International Alert Line and the Retirement Gap Tends to Enlarge, people.com.cn, November 1, 2013.

19. Several Important Issues of China's Social Security System in Urgent Need of Solutions – Interview with Zheng Bingwen, Director of the World Social Security Research Center and Director of the Institute of Latin American Studies, Party and Government Forum, Issue 3, 2011.

医保、新农
13
费用审核　政策咨

Education, Health and Human Resources

Education and health shape the quality of a nation. The former determines the cultural and scientific quality of citizens, while the latter affects their physical quality. Both factors form the basis for the productivity and development potential of humans. Complete investigations, of course, should include moral quality. Education and health mentioned here are in their narrow sense, with the former focusing on formal schooling and the latter nutrition and health care.

The Chinese government has always attached great importance to developing education and health causes. Since the founding of New China, especially during China's reform and opening-up, China has seen universalization of compulsory education in an all-round way and basic education taken to a new level. Vocational education has developed rapidly, leading to notable improvements in the structure and quality of increased labor. Education and higher learning have achieved remarkable development, making outstanding contributions to talent cultivation, scientific and technological innovations and social services. Continuing education has advanced, providing society with diverse approaches to

learning. The modern education system has begun to take shape and China has grown into a power in education and human resources. In terms of health, the medical security system has improved and the total quantity of health resources has increased. Medical services have become much more accessible to the public, immunization work targeting various infectious diseases has produced notable results, and citizen awareness of safety, nutrition and health care have increased now that the problems of food and clothing are solved. These achievements certainly didn't come easy, and China still lags far behind developed countries in many fields and has a long way to go before it changes its large population into a high-value talent pool.

Reform and Development in Education

Changes in the Education System and School Management in the Two Decades Prior to Reform

In the long run, education is the foundation of national development. After the end of the Cultural Revolution, education was one of the first institutions to be restored, including the college entrance examination system, key school system and school management system. The set of systems has undergone substantial changes since the 1980s. As for administrative power, the principle that local authorities assumed responsibility for education, which was administered at

The teaching principles about the integrated development of morality, intelligence, physique and labour were implemented in many rural schools of China from 1978 to 1988.

The two-month tour for the mobile China Museum of Science and Technology in Guangxi Province started from the National Culture Square in Mulao Autonomous County, Luocheng City on June 30th, 2014. The places for science and technology practice were provided for people, especially for the students from primary schools and middle schools, to enjoy the interactive and experimental science education.

different levels, was established for basic education. Schools of higher learning were gradually delegated to authorities at lower levels, adjusted and merged. The situation in which schools were run by different departments that were separated by administrative barriers was fundamentally reversed giving schools a higher level of autonomy. Rural education saw the transformation from school running at various levels to dominance by county-level education authorities, with the source of input increasingly from governments rather than agricultural surtax and town-level fiscal budgets.

As for the school management, the system of key schools for compulsory education was gradually canceled after being restored for a period of time.

But since the middle 1990s, 1,000 "demonstration regular high schools" have emerged, with the phenomena such as school selection and corresponding charges not improving much. College education received unprecedented attention, and Project 211 and Project 98520 were successively launched, with a number of super-large colleges dominated by administrative authorities springing up. That came with drastic increases in land and supporting resources occupied by colleges and ever-expanding enrollment since 1999 intended for popularization of higher education.

After China explicitly set the goal of developing a socialist market economy in its economic reforms of 1992, a heated discussion centering on the marketization and industrialization of education arose in education circles, and the policy of charging for non-compulsory education was introduced (supplemented by diverse support and award policies). Raising funds for education through multiple channels filled the fiscal input gap and resulted in a diverse composition of educational funds. Funds from social groups and individual citizens, funds donated and raised in society, as well as non-fiscal educational funds including tuition fees, sundry fees and other revenue once made up more than 30% of the total funds for education. Private education developed as well, and school management enterprises boomed. To meet needs for expansion, many schools, schools of higher learning in particular, had to bear heavy debt burdens. The marketization and industrialization of education deviated from the concept of education as a public product. Furthermore, parents' high expectations of their only children, increasing employment pressure and competition among schools for bragging rights over university placement has led to growing stress for both students and parents. Quality educational resources constantly flowed into the regions and schools with better foundations, resulting in severe imbalances in resource allocation as well as widening gaps among regions and between urban and rural areas. Some areas, especially poor rural areas, reported rising dropout rates among youngsters. The problem of educational inequality has attracted increasing attention.

The latest reform and development of education were introduced on the press conference by Ministry of Education on Jan. 25th, 2006.

China experienced great achievements as well as problems in education during the two decades before its reform and opening-up. As for achievements, the gross enrollment ratio in education at various levels, except primary schools, improved greatly. Table 5-1-1 shows that from 1992 to 2002, the gross enrollment ratio for junior high schools rose from 71.8% to 90.0%, senior high schools from 26.0% to 42.8%, and schools of higher learning from 3.9% to 15.0%; The two goals, i.e. making nine-year compulsory education universally available and basically eliminating illiteracy among young and middle-aged adults, were initially realized. Pre-school education and special education made great headway. Vocational education of all kinds and continuing education realized all-round development. Higher education experienced significant expansion, with about 11 million college students at campuses in 2000 and the number of postgraduates rising to 301,000 from only 22,000 in 1980. Foreign cxchanges and cooperation in education expanded, with the numbers of Chinese students studying abroad and foreign students studying in China both growing. Education reform advanced and legal construction produced fruitful results. Conditions for school management were improved to a degree, as was the quality of schooling.

Besides problems arising from marketization and industrialization, China also lagged far behind developed economies in the development of education, which was reflected mainly in the years per capita of schooling years for citizens, as well as school funding and management. Compared with developed economies, the years of schooling per capita in China was still at a low level, although it almost doubled from the period around 1980. This will be detailed later when we cover the general conditions of China's human resources. As for school management systems, China was different from developed economies.

China achieved the goal that educational expenditure accounted for 4% of GDP in 2012, and made efforts to consolidate the achievement.

Governments centralized functions of school management and administration and public schools occupied an absolutely dominant position. In 2001, private education institutions at various levels reported 5,660,000 students on campus, accounting for only 2.5% of the total. On a specific term, the students in private primary schools, middle schools and schools of higher learning comprised 1.5%, 3.0% and 9.0% of the national total, respectively. In 1996, the students in private primary schools in the US, South Korea and France represented 12%, 1% and 15% of their national total, respectively. The students in private middle schools in these three countries made up 10%, 38% and 20% of their national total, respectively. In 1999, vocational private schools of higher learning in the same three countries accounted for 7.4%, 86.0% and 26.3% of the total number of students in such schools, respectively. Academic private schools of higher learning comprised 34.5%, 76.5% and 9.8% of the total number of students in such schools, respectively. Compared with developed economies, China spent less on education. In 2001, China's spending on education represented only 4.83% of GDP, compared with an average of 5.8% in OECD countries and 6%-7% in South Korea, US and Canada in 1998. In 2001, China's fiscal spending education made up 3.19% of GDP, 2.2 percentage points lower than the level of the US in 1997 and also lower than the levels in Brazil (4.63%), Malaysia (4.49%) and Thailand (4.27%) in 1998. Governments contributed a small portion of funds for compulsory education. In 2001, only 63.2% of the total spending on compulsory education came from fiscal funds. Less than 60% of the education funds for junior high schools were sourced from government budgets, and the figure for primary schools was lower than 70%. By contrast, fiscal funds for primary school, middle school and post-middle school education in OECD countries was at 90.9% in 1998.

Highlights in China's Educational System Reform and Development in the 21st Century

In the 21st century, especially since the 16th National Congress of the

CPC, China has deeply implemented the strategy of developing China through science and education and strengthening the country through human resource development. As a result, education as a strategic priority in China's development agenda has been consolidated and intensified, and historical achievements were made in education.

—China's fiscal spending in education has improved, fulfilling the goal of comprising 4% of GDP. The *Outlines for China's Education Reform and Development* released in 1993 explicitly noted that "China shall gradually

Table 5-1-1
Gross Enrollment Ratio in Education at Various Levels in China

Year	Three-year pre-school Education	Primary school Education	Junior High School Education	Senior High School Education		Higher Education
	Computed Based on Corresponding School Ages in Different Areas	Computed Based on Corresponding School Ages in Different Areas	12-14 Years Old	15-17 years old		18-22 Years Old
				Before Career	Full Population	
1991		109.5	69.7	23.9		3.5
1992		109.4	71.8	22.6	26.0	3.9
1993		107.3	73.1	24.1	28.4	5.0
1994		108.7	73.8	26.2	30.7	6.0
1995		106.6	78.4	28.8	33.6	7.2
1996		105.7	82.4	31.4	38.0	8.3
1997		104.9	87.1	33.8	40.6	9.1
1998		104.3	87.3	34.4	40.7	9.8
1999		104.3	88.6	35.8	41.0	10.5

2000		104.6	88.6	38.2	42.8	12.5
2001		104.5	88.7	38.6	42.8	13.3
2002	36.8	107.5	90.0	38.4	42.8	15.0
2003	37.4	107.2	92.7	42.1	43.8	17.0
2004	40.8	106.6	94.1	46.5	48.1	19.0
2005	41.4	106.4	95.0	50.9	52.7	21.0
2006	42.5	106.3	97.0	57.7	59.8	22.0
2007	44.6	106.2	98.0		66.0	23.0
2008	47.3	105.7	98.5		74.0	23.3
2009	50.9	104.8	99.0		79.2	24.2
2010	56.6	104.6	100.1		82.5	26.5
2011	62.3	104.2	100.1		84.0	26.9
2012	64.5	99.9*	102.1		85.0	30.0

* Net enrollment ratio

Data source: *Education is the Foundation of National Development in the Long Run—Review of China's Education Reform since the 16th CPC National Congress (2002-2012)*, compiled by Yuan Guiren, published by the People's Publishing House in 2011; CERNET; Official website of the Ministry of Education.

increase the proportion of fiscal spending on education (including allocations for education by governments at all levels, urban and rural education surcharges, enterprises' spending on running primary and middle schools, and tax exemptions of enterprises run by schools) to GDP, which shall reach 4% at the end of the 20th century, the average level in developing countries in the 1980s. Planning, fiscal and taxation authorities shall formulate corresponding policies and earnestly implement the policies." However, a skewed view of development, which highlighted pure pursuit of economic growth, led local governments to make GDP a major indicator for assessing political performance. The prevalence of pragmatism and unclear boundaries between government and market functions

Table 5-1-2 National Education Spending Unit: RMB 100 Million		
	National Education Spending	National Fiscal Spending on Education
2002	5480.0	3491.4
2003	6208.3	3850.6
2004	7242.6	4465.9
2005	8418.8	5161.1
2006	9815.3	6348.4
2007	12148.1	8280.2
2008	14500.7	10449.6
2009	16502.7	12231.1
2010	19561.8	14670.1
2011	23869.3	18586.7
2012	27696.0	21984.0

Figure 5-1-1
Growth in National Education Spending

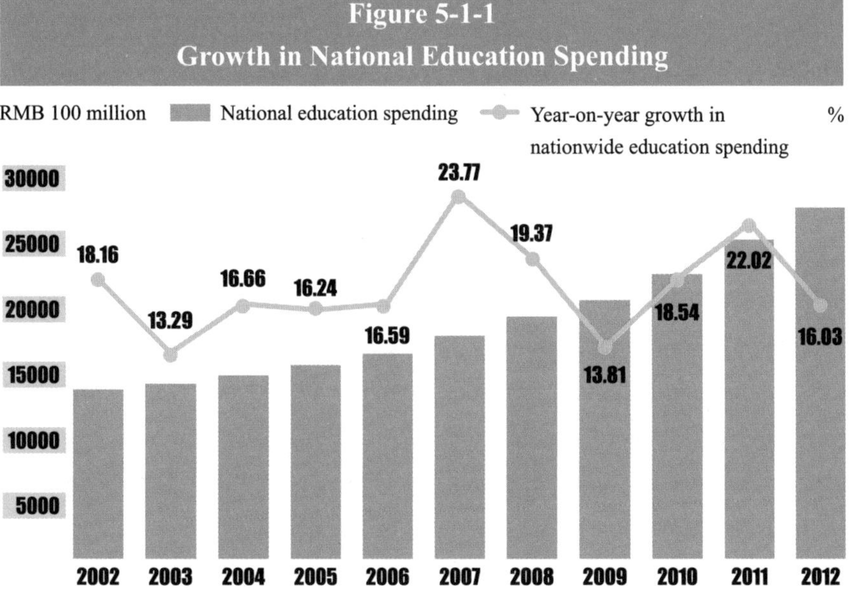

Figure 5-1-2
Growth in China's Fiscal Spending on Education

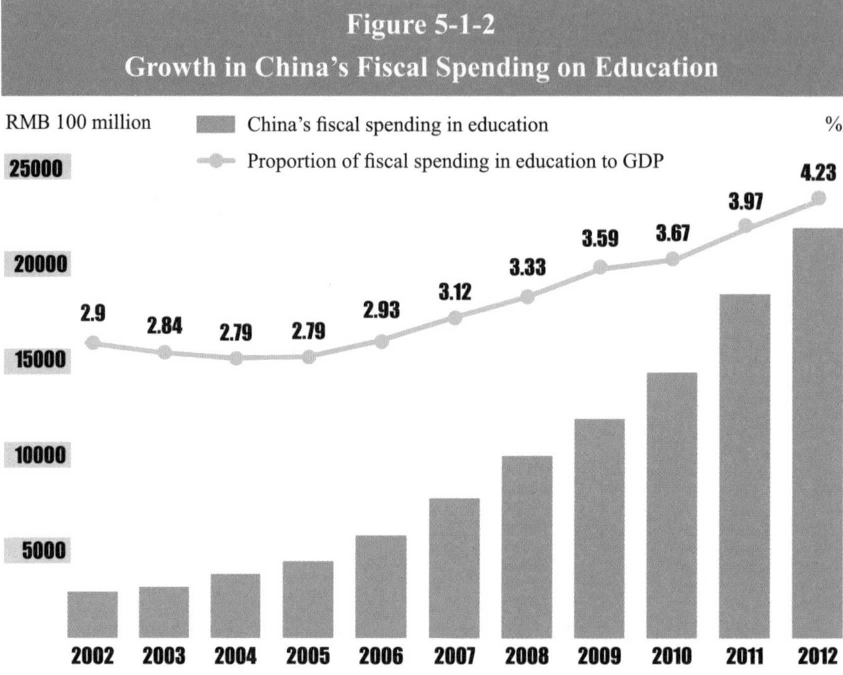

added to the limitations on increasing fiscal spending on education. Prior to 2006, China's fiscal spending on education had long been less than 3% of GDP and was seriously unbalanced. Since the 16th National Congress of the CPC, social causes including education have received great attention. The *Outline of the Eleventh Five-year Plan for National Economic and Social Development* passed at the fourth session of the 10th NPC and the *Decision of the CPC Central Committee on Numerous Key Issues Concerning Building Socialism and a Harmonious Society* made at the sixth plenary session of the 16th Central Committee of the CPC held in 2006 both reiterated the target of 4%, and nationwide fiscal spending on education began to exceed 3% and improved year after year from then on. Afterwards, Chinese leaders repeatedly stressed the "Three Priorities" (to prioritize education in economic and social development plans, prioritize fiscal spending on education and prioritize satisfaction of needs arising from developing education and human resources with public resources), requiring the immediate establishment of a scientific and regulated system of fiscal support. According to the *Outline of China's Medium and Long-term Plan on Education Reform and Development (2010–2020)* developed in the spirit of the 17th National Congress of the CPC, "efforts shall be made to improve the proportion of nationwide fiscal spending on education to GDP, which shall reach 4% in 2012." Although China's fiscal spending on education will reach or exceed 4% in 2012, it will still lag far behind developed economies in this regard.

—The education reform has been moving forward, with a big advance in fairness. As for administration, governments at different levels have clearer responsibilities and authorities in administering education at various levels. Compulsory education is directed by the State Council, planned and implemented by provincial governments and mainly managed by county-level governments. Vocational education, under the leadership of the State Council, is administered at different levels, with local governments taking a dominant position and various

A school library was also built in the most remote rural primary school of Binzhou City, Shandong Province.

social forces playing a part. Higher education is administered at both the central and provincial levels, with provincial governments playing a major role. As for school management, the relationship between governments and schools is better defined, with the autonomy of schools in management secured.A landscape in which public schools have a dominant position while developing together with private schools has come into being. As for spending, the fiscal system for public education has been put in place, and governments have a strong responsibility in securing public education. The cost-sharing mechanism for non-compulsory education has been improved and a system in which compulsory education is wholly financed by governments and funds for non-compulsory education are mainly from government budgets and other channels has taken shape. Education has opened further to the outside world, with foreign exchanges growing and Confucius Institutes increasingly influential. Meanwhile, free compulsory education was fully realized in rural and urban areas successively in 2006 and 2008, benefiting 160 million children of school age. A complete system for subsidizing students from poor families has been initially established for every stage from pre-school to postgraduate education. Substantial progress has been made in balancing development of compulsory education. Arbitrary charges for education have been curbed and rights of the children of rural migrant workers living in cities and the disabled to education has been guaranteed. Public education resources are tilting toward rural areas, remote poor areas and ethnic minority areas. Construction of rural boarding schools, reconstruction of junior middle school buildings in central and western rural areas, safety projects for nationwide primary and middle school buildings, reconstruction of the rural schools weak in compulsory education and some other projects launched since 2004 have greatly improved the conditions in rural schools.

—Education has been increasingly popularized with higher quality. Pre-school education has gathered pace. Compulsory education has achieved a historic leap forward. Senior high school education is more popularized and higher education is more accessible to the public. Table 6-1-1 shows that from

2002 to 2012, the gross enrollment ratio in pre-school education rose from 36.8% to 64.5%. With the gross enrollment ratio up more than 10%, junior high school education was fully popularized along with primary school education. The figure for senior high school education grew from 42.8% to 85.0% and college education from 15% to 30%. A new curriculum system that meets the requirements of quality education has been basically established in primary and middle schools, resulting in improvements in the comprehensive quality of students. The strategic position of vocational education has become more important, and the school management model has taken initial shape. Higher education has shifted from extensive expansion to intensive development, with construction of high-level universities and key disciplines obviously strengthened, yet college graduates are having increasing difficulties in finding jobs. Ethnic minority education is enjoying a higher standard, with policy support and partner assistance producing notable effects. The teaching pool is expanding and education is increasingly informatized.

Goals and Measures for Deepening Education Reform

There have been profound changes in China's education situation. With 260 million students, 16 million teachers and 520,000 schools, China has the world's biggest education system, with increasingly complex organizations, diversified structures and differentiated levels of schools of different kinds as well as personalized appeal for education among the public. Large-scale population flows as well as economic globalization and informatization have had a substantial impact on the philosophy and methods of education, while the accelerated development of the economy and all-round transformation of society has raised the bar for the quality, role and international competitiveness of education. To achieve modernization, China must prioritize the modernization of education. The 18th CPC National Congress explicitly noted that education modernization will be basically realized by 2020. It's an arduous task to modernize the world's biggest education system as a whole.

The *Outline of China's Long and Medium-term Plan on Education Reform and Development (2010-2020)* released by the Chinese government in 2010 included pre-school education in the plan and proposed basic popularization of pre-school education. It required alleviation of academic burdens on primary and middle school students, and allowed entrance to examinations for education at a higher level by the children of rural migrant workers in cities. It called for efforts to gradually implement free secondary vocational education, accelerate separation between governments and schools and between school administration and running, deepen reform in the professional titles of primary and middle school teachers, advance college entrance examinations by category, and address discrimination against private school teachers. Regarding school selection resulting from gaps among different schools, which has been criticized for a long time, the outline stated that no key schools or classes should be arranged at the compulsory education stage. It also proposed to reconstruct weak schools at a faster pace, improve the quality of teaching staff, reasonably allocate enrollment quotas of quality ordinary senior middle schools and quality secondary vocational schools to the junior middle schools in respective regions, and develop private education for more opportunities while ensuring enrollment of school-age children in nearby public schools. The outline aimed to solve problems related to balanced development and education equity. The main goals it put forward are seen in Table 5-1-3.

The *Decision of the CPC Central Committee on Numerous Major Issues Related to Comprehensively Deepening the Reform* made by the third plenary session of the 18th CPC Central Committee in 2013 proposed to deepen the comprehensive reform in the education field, and made comprehensive deployment centered on promoting the all-around development of students and education equity. Regarding the entrance examination system, whichhas attracted the most attention from both parents and schools, the decision stated that "efforts will be made to promote the reform of the examination and college admission system, explore an operational mechanism in which college

Table 5-1-3
Main Goals for Comprehensively Building Education in a Well-off Society

Indicator	Unit	2009	2015	2020
Pre-school education				
Number of kindergarten students	10,000 people	2658	3400	4000
Gross enrollment ratio of one-year preschool education	%	74.0	85.0	95.0
Gross enrollment ratio of two-year preschool education	%	65.0	70.0	80.0
Gross enrollment ratio of three-year preschool education	%	50.9	60.0	70.0
Nine-year compulsory education				
Schools at campus	10,000 people	15772	16100	16500
Retention ratio	%	90.8	93.0	95.0
Senior middle school education*				
Schools at campus	10,000 people	4624	4500	4700
Gross enrollment ratio	%	79.2	87.0	90.0
Vocational education				
Students in secondary vocational schools	10,000 people	2179	2250	2350
Students in higher vocational schools	10,000 people	1280	1390	1480
Higher education**				
Students at campus	10,000 people	2979	3350	3550
Schools at campus	10,000 people	2826	3080	3300
Including: postgraduates	10,000 people	140	170	200
Gross enrollment ratio	%	24.2	36.0	40.0
Continuing education				
Continuing education for employed persons	10,000 person times	16600	29000	35000

Note: *Including the number of students in secondary vocational schools; ** Including the number of students in higher vocational schools.

The Decision by the Third Plenary Session of the 18th Central Committee of the Communist Party of China, proposed the reform of college entrance examination system that would impact on millions of Chinese students.

admission and examination are separated to a certain extent, in which students have multiple opportunities in the college entrance examinations, colleges admit students independently according to law, professional institutions organize for implementation, the government enforces macro control, and society participates in the supervision, so as to eradicate the drawback of 'one's fate being determined by an examination'. A school district system in which students enter schools within their respective districts throughout their nine-year compulsory education without taking any examinations will be implemented. Efforts will be made to promote academic proficiency tests and comprehensive quality evaluation in junior and senior high schools, administer categorized tests and open admissions for vocational school entrance, and gradually establish a comprehensive evaluation and diversified college admission mechanism based on the results in the unified national entrance examinations for regular institutions of higher learning and proficiency test results in high schools. Efforts will also be made to explore ways to reduce the number of courses in the unified national examinations, with a mixture of social and natural sciences, have open-to-all foreign language tests several times a year, and to unify credits among regular higher-learning institutions, higher vocational schools and adult colleges, thus broadening the channels for lifelong learning." If such policies are actually implemented and smoothly advanced, the examination-oriented education system and the situation of one's fate being determined by an examination will be greatly changed. 2013

Reform of the Medical System and Development of the Medical and Health Cause

The Tortuous Course of China's Medical System Reform in the New Period

Similar to education reform, China's medical reform has also undergone a tortuous process, with problems concentrated in excessive marketization. It can be said that medical reform didn't take a right path until years ago, and this serves as another reflection of China's cautious exploration of reform.

In 2014, the reform of medical and health care system in China drew much attention during the two sessions.

The State Council approved and put forward the *Report on Numerous Policy Issues Concerning Health Care Reform* made by the Ministry of Health on April 25, 1985, marking the official kickoff of China's medical reform. Regarding the slow advance in health care and the imbalance between medical services on one hand and economic construction and public demand on the other, the report suggested setting up medical institutions through multiple channels, at multiple levels and in multiple forms, expanding the autonomy of medical institutions, raising medical charges and increasing benefits for medical staff to arouse the enthusiasm of every side. As a result of the reform, medical institutions were better motivated to earn income, and government spending on health care took up a smaller part while residents' medical expenses rose quickly.

The State Council released *Several Opinions on Deepening the Health Care Reform* in September 1992, noting that efforts should be made to expand fundraising channels for medical services, improve the compensation mechanism, introduce reforms in the medical service price system and adjust

The annual per capita medical expense has increased more than 30 times in the 26 years as an increasing burden of people.

charging structures based on the law of values. Basic preventative health care services should be ensured, and restrictions on special preventative healthcare service prices should be loosened. By this point, the reform had initially shown its market orientation.

After the 14th CPC National Congress clearly set the goal of developing a socialist market economy for China's economic system reform in 1992, market-oriented reforms quickly extended from the economy to several fields previously dominated by the government, including education, health care and housing. The State Council released the *Decision on Health Care Reform and Development and the Decision on Establishing the Urban Employees' Basic Medical Insurance System* in 1997 and 1998, respectively, which proposed to reform the medical security system for urban employees,establish a medical insurance system that combines social pooling with individual accounts, and put in place cooperative medical systems in diverse forms in most rural areas under the principle of public support for private responsibility and voluntary participation. The reform quickly impacted the property system in public hospitals. The *Guiding Opinions for Medical Reform in Urban Areas* released in 2000 suggested establishing a new system for administration of medical institutions by categories through "encouraging cooperation and merging among medical institutions of various types" and"jointly setting up medical service groups and loosening restrictions on medical service prices charged by profit-oriented medical institutions". Therefore, the focus of medical reform at this stage was to marketize medical services and make medical institutions run like enterprises. This resulted in increased enthusiasm by public hospitals for profits, prominent contradictions between doctors and patients, contracting public medical services, surging medical expenses, excessively heavy burdens on individuals and unavailability of medical security to a considerable number of people. The deficiencies and after-effects were seen in the SARS crisis that broke out in 2003, and the state of health care and the direction of the medical reform aroused great attention and heated discussions in Chinese society.

According to the *Decision of the CPC Central Committee on Several Important Issues in Constructing of a Socialist Harmonious Society* made in 2006, "The public welfare nature of public medical services should be kept, and efforts should be made to deepen medical reform, strengthen governments' responsibilities, tighten supervision and administration and establish a basic health care system that covers both urban and rural residents, so as to provide the people with safe, effective, convenient and affordable public health care and basic medical services." In line with the principle and orientation, a new medical reform plan, namely *Opinions of the CPC Central Committee and the State Council on Deepening the Reform of the Medical and Health Care System*, was launched in 2009 after three years of full consideration and extensive solicitation of public opinions. The plan held the basic philosophy of providing all citizens with basic medical services as public products and intensifying governments' responsibility in the basic medical system. It set the short-term goal of "effectively reducing medical expenses of residents", and the long-term goal of "establishing a basic medical system that covers both urban and rural residents, so as to provide the people with safe, effective, convenient and affordable medical services". It described the short-term roadmap for deepening medical reform, made clear five priority areas for the following three years and called for realization of the public welfare nature of public health care and efforts to solve problems that attract public attention. The five priorities include providing medical insurance for all to relieve the medical expense burdens on residents, initially establishing the national essential drug system to reduce essential drug expenses of residents, improving grassroots medical service systems to make medical services accessible to the people, promoting equalization of basic public health care services to help people avoid disease, advancing pilot projects in public hospital reform by improving service quality and efficiency, and shortening patients' waiting times and realizing mutual recognition of checkup results among medical institutions at the same level. The five priorities were detailed and implemented in the *Short-term Plan for Implementation of Medical Reform (2009-2011)*

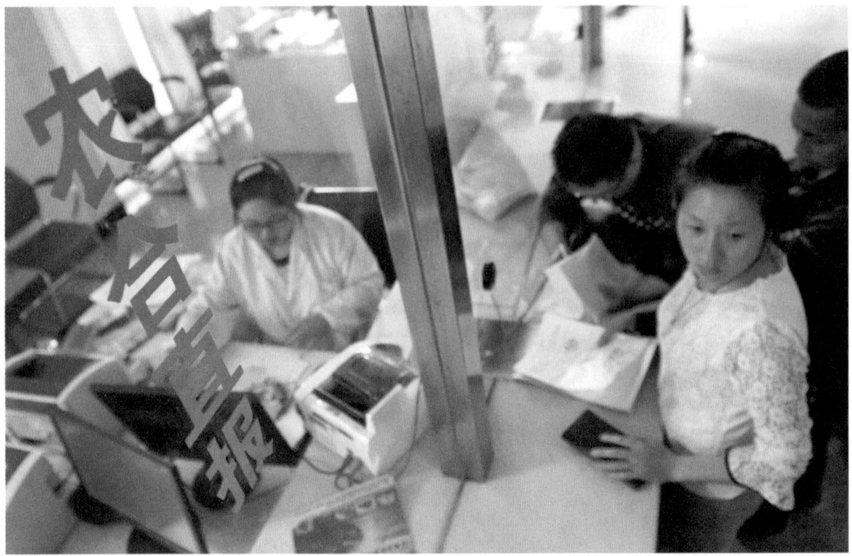

The fast promotion of the "new reform of medical and health care system" in recent years. The national information platform of new rural cooperative medical system opened in 2013.

released at the same time. It can be concluded that the new medical reform is a systematic project that covers a wide scope and adhering to the public welfare nature of basic medical services is one of the themes.

Main Achievements of Medical Reform

After three to four years of efforts, medical reform has gathered pace, with the framework for a basic medical system with Chinese characteristics coming into shape.

First, a basic medical security system has been basically established, marking a critical step towards the goal of "ensuring all people enjoy the right to medical services". By 2011, the number of subscribers to medical insurance for employees, medical insurance for urban residents and new rural cooperative medical insurance exceeded 1.3 billion, representing more than 95% of China's total population. Launched in 2002, the new rural cooperative medical scheme covered 832 million people in 2011, or a coverage rate of 97.5%. The per capita fundraising standard increased from RMB 30 in 2003 to RMB 246 in 2011, and beneficiaries grew from 76 million visits in 2004 to 1.32 billion visits in 2011. More than 70% of the hospitalization expenses that fall into the policy scope can be reimbursed, with the maximum amount of reimbursement up to RMB 80,000. In 2010, the catastrophic disease insurance system under the new rural cooperative medical scheme was implemented, and by the end of 2011, nearly 300,000 patients suffering from eight catastrophic diseases including childhood leukemia, congenital heart disease and end-stage kidney disease were reimbursed, with the actual reimbursement ratio averaging 65%. In 2012, 12 frequently occurring serious diseases, including lung cancer, esophagus cancer and stomach cancer, were included in the pilot range of serious disease insurance system in rural areas, with the reimbursement ratio reaching 90% at most. In 2013, the third plenary session of the 18th Central Committee of the CPC required

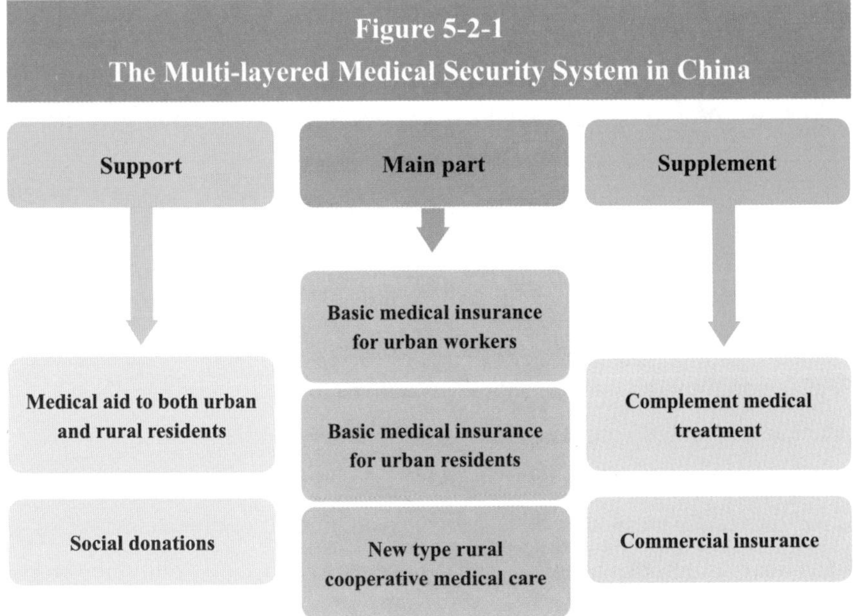

accelerated construction of a mechanism to provide insurance and aid in treating major diseases, according to which six ministries and commissions including the National Development and Reform Commission released the *Guiding Opinions on the Supplementary Insurance of Major Diseases for Urban and Rural Residents*, deciding to kick off pilot projects of major disease insurance for urban and rural residents in 2014.

Second, a national essential drug system has been put in place, and the new mechanism for running grass-roots medical institutions has gradually taken shape. By 2011, "zero-profit" sales of essential drugs covered all the grassroots medical institutions run by governments, and the national essential drug system was built from scratch and extended to village clinics, grassroots medical institutions not run by governments and public hospitals. As a result, prices of essential drugs have dropped by 30% or above on average. Meanwhile, comprehensive reform in grassroots medical institutions has advanced and special fiscal subsidies and subsidies for current revenue and expenditure deficits have been implemented. Comprehensive evaluation of performance and performance-related pays has been introduced, and a new mechanism for operation has been established step by step.

Third, the grassroots medical service system has been effectively consolidated, and the goal of "strengthening grassroots medical services" has been initially achieved. Since 2009, the central government has allocated more than RMB 47 billion of fiscal funds to support construction of business rooms in grassroots medical institutions. It has also initiated construction of talent teams for grassroots medical services with general practitioners as the focus, arranging 36,000 workers in grassroots medical institutions to receive trainings for general practitioners, and offering free fostering of medical students according to orders from rural areas in central and west China. More than 10,000 talent individuals were fostered for grass-roots rural medical institutions in central and west China. After years of efforts, grassroots areas have experienced a steadily improving level of basic medical services and the enhanced quality of grassroots medical institutions. The new mechanism runs smoothly. Medical institutions have strong capabilities to serve the people and rural doctor teams have become basically stable while gradually optimizing.

Fourth, public health care projects have been implemented, and public health services for urban and rural residents have been increasingly equalized. China provides all of its citizens with 41 items of free basic public health services under ten major categories, with the charging standards raised from a per capita level of RMB 15 in 2009 to RMB 25 in 2011, and the number of beneficiaries is growing. Regarding special diseases, key population groups and special areas, China has introduced major public health projects, including hospital delivery subsidies for rural women, hepatitis B re-vaccination for those under the age of 15, folic acid supplementation for rural women at pre-pregnancy and early pregnancy stages, free surgeries for poor cataract patients and cervical cancer and breast cancer screening for rural women of appropriate age, benefiting nearly 200 million people.

The national system for basic drugs was initially established in China, driving the prices of basic drugs down.

Fifth, pilot projects of the reform in public hospitals have been advanced in an orderly manner, with useful experience accumulated. Since 2010, 17 state-level pilot cities and 37 provincial-level pilot areas have launched pilot projects of reform in public hospitals, improving service systems, innovating in mechanisms and intensifying internal management. In 2012, 311 counties (cities) nationwide kicked off pilot projects of comprehensive reform in county-level public hospitals, and improved mechanisms for management, compensation, personnel, pricing, procurement and regulation, focusing on changing the situation in which a hospital subsidizes its medical services with overly expensive drug prescriptions. Efforts have been made to popularize clinical pathway management, mutual recognition of checkup results among medical institutions at the same level, doctor-appointment services, time-phased outpatient services, outpatient services during weekends and holidays as well as quality nursing services, so as to lower medical expenses, make medical services more accessible to the public, improve service quality and effectively ease the tension between

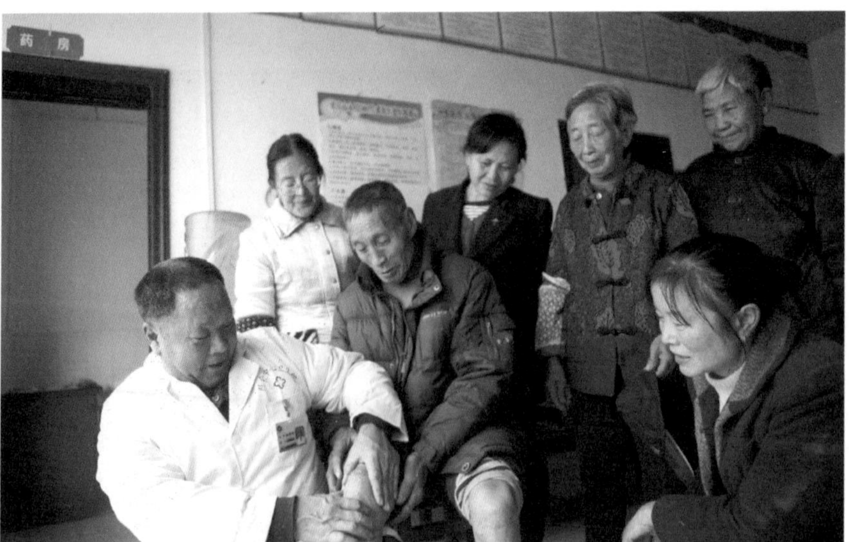

Villagers suffering from common ailments can enjoy basic public health service in their own village.

doctors and patients. Policies aimed to encourage hospital management via social forces have been further improved. In 2012, the number of private hospitals increased by 4,383, or 81.1%, to 9,786 from 5,403 in 2008, before medical reform was introduced, and the proportion of the total number of hospitals went up from 27.4% to 42.2%. Meanwhile, the number of public hospitals decreased by 925 to 13,384 from 14,309, and the proportion dropped to 57.8% from 72.6%. *Several Opinions of the State Council on Accelerating the Development of the Health Service Industry*, released in September 2013, called for vigorous efforts to develop medical services and accelerated formation of a diverse landscape of hospital management. To follow the requirements of the third plenary session of the 18th Central Committee of the CPC on encouraging hospital management by social forces, the National Health and Family Planning Commission and the State Administration of Traditional Chinese Medicine jointly released the *Several Opinions on Accelerating the Development of Hospital Managementby Social Forces* in early 2014, putting forward several concrete policies to address the challenges facing hospital management via social forces. It is expected that by 2015, non-public medical institutions will account for about 20% of the total number of hospital beds and service volumes.

Sixth, in terms of prevention and control of serious diseases, key infectious diseases and endemics that pose a severe threat to residents' health have been effectively controlled, and China has improved capability to respond to health emergencies. By the end of 2010, there were about 760,000 HIV-infected people and AIDS patients in China, well below the objective of controlling the number of HIV/AIDS infected people at a level lower than 1.5 million. The national pulmonary tuberculosis mortality rate fell to 66/100,000, meeting the pulmonary tuberculosis control target of the UN Millennium Development Goals in advance. Schistosomiasis patients numbered about 326,000, down 61.3% from 2004, and all the Chinese counties with prevalence of schistosomiasis fulfilled the objective of epidemic control. In 2004, a direct online reporting system for infectious diseases was put into use. Since 2007, the category of planned vaccines has increased from six to 14, with the diseases prevented rising to 15 from seven and the groups expanding from children to adults, which effectively lowered the incidence of infectious diseases. At the State level, the objective of eliminating iodine deficiency disorders has been achieved, and the incidence of Kashin-Beck disease, Keshan disease and fluorosis has been under effective control. An emergency management mechanism at the state, provincial, prefectural and county levels has been established, while a coordination mechanism among multiple sectors for response of sudden outbreaks has taken shape. Twenty-seven state-level health emergency response teams respectively in fields such as infectious disease control, first aid, poisoning response and nuclear radiation response have been set up. Sudden outbreaks, including SARS, H1N1 flu, pestis and human infections with bird flu, have been effectively controlled and emergency medical aid has been organized for natural disasters like the massive

Figure 5-2-2
Proportion of China's Health Expenses to GDP

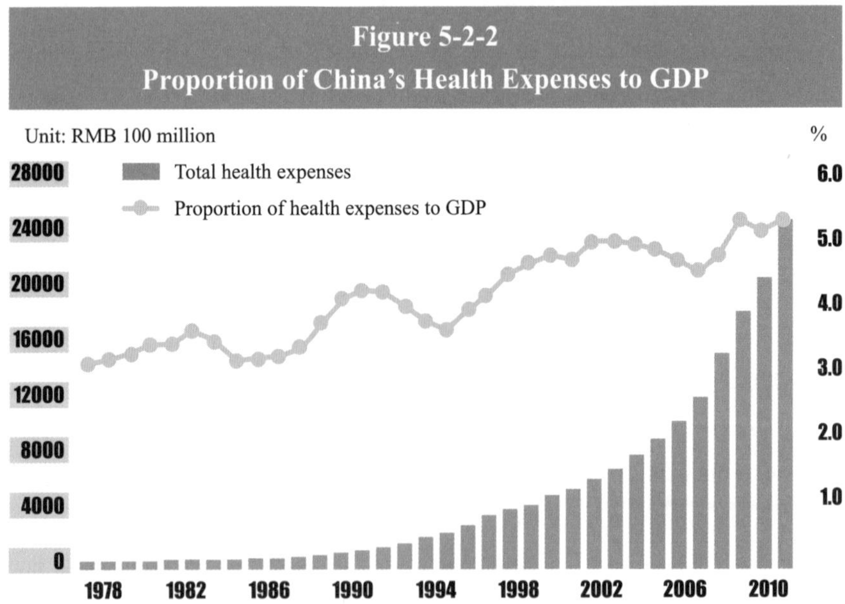

Data source: State Council Information Office of China: *Medical and Health Services in China* (White Paper), December 2012.

Figure 5-2-3

Composition of Funds Raised for Health Expenses in China

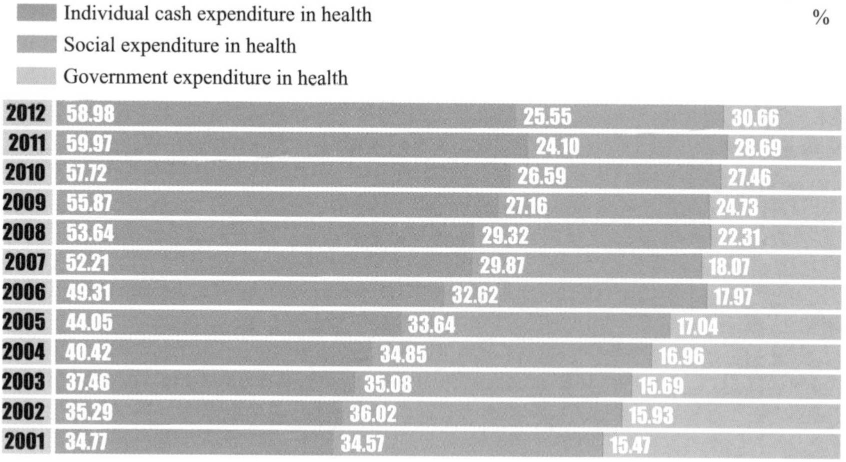

Individual cash expenditure in health

Social expenditure in health

Government expenditure in health

%

Year			
2012	58.98	25.55	30.66
2011	59.97	24.10	28.69
2010	57.72	26.59	27.46
2009	55.87	27.16	24.73
2008	53.64	29.32	22.31
2007	52.21	29.87	18.07
2006	49.31	32.62	17.97
2005	44.05	33.64	17.04
2004	40.42	34.85	16.96
2003	37.46	35.08	15.69
2002	35.29	36.02	15.93
2001	34.77	34.57	15.47

Data source: State Council Information Office of China: *Medical and Health Services in China* (White Paper), December 2012.

earthquake in Wenchuan, Sichuan Province as well as the earthquake in Yushu, Qinghai Province and landslide in Zhouqu, Gansu Province, protecting residents' lives and health.

Seventh, the Patriotic Health Campaign has drawn more public participation. In 2012, 153 state-level hygienic cities, 32 state-level hygienic districts and 456 state-level hygienic towns (counties) were established and the rates of access to tap water and hygienic toilets in rural areas reached 72.1% and 69.2%, respectively, which has played a big role in lowering the threat from infectious diseases and improve residents' health conditions. The capability to regulate food and drug safety has been enhanced and great efforts have been made to develop standards and safety plans, conduct risk monitoring, crack down on illegal acts, advance construction of electronic regulation systems and put in place systems for product quality tracing and safety emergency response. Policies devised to support and promote development of traditional Chinese medicine have been implemented, and traditional Chinese medicine has played a bigger role in public health, basic medical services and prevention and treatment of serious and complicated diseases. Construction of scientific and technological teams has been further strengthened and international cooperation on health has been deepened.

Basic Measures to Deepen Medical Reform During the 12th Five-year Plan Period

China's reforms since 2009 demonstrate that the new medical reform has a correct direction, a clear path and vigorous measures. It has produced notable effects, particularly at the grassroots level, and made medical services more equitable, accessible and affordable. Medical reform has played an increasingly big role in promoting economic and social development.

However, China's ongoing medical reform still falls short of public expectations. (1) The reform in public hospitals has moved slowly, and the

The "blacklist" system of food and drugs will be officially established in China.

operation mechanism and performance assessment mechanism in line with public nature and functional requirements have not been put in place. Salaries for hospital staffs and expenses for operation rely mainly on services charges and there are conflicts of interest between doctors and patients. (2) Allocation of medical resources is not reasonable, with quality resources concentrated in big cities and hospitals while grassroots medical institutions have few high-quality staff and poor service capabilities. (3) A reasonable pre-triage system hasn't been established. As a result, most people still resort to big hospitals for treatment of common and frequently occurring diseases, and the problem of access to medical services remains prominent. (4) The reimbursement mechanism to change the way in which a hospital subsidizes its medical services with overly expensive drug prescriptions has not been established. (5) Drug production, procurement and sales orders remain chaotic, and problems including artificially high drug prices, commercial bribery and drug rebate have not been properly addressed. (6) There are still many obstacles facing hospital management in the private sector and the landscape in which hospitals are managed through multiple channels has not been established.

Regarding outstanding problems in the medical and health field, the State Council released the *Plan on Deepening Medical Reform during the 12th Five-year Plan Period and Implementation Plan* in March 2012, requiring adherence to the core philosophy of providing basic health care for all, the basic principle of ensuring basic services, improving such services at the grassroots level and establishing the effective mechanisms and the guideline of putting disease prevention first, making rural areas the focus of work and supporting both traditional Chinese medicine and Western medicine. With the aim of safeguarding and increasing the health of all and with the core being the building of a basic medical and health system, the plan calls for comprehensive deployment with clear priorities and orderly advances to further deepen the reform in medical security, medical services, public health, drug supply and regulation. The plan encourages breakthroughs in the development of medical insurance for all and

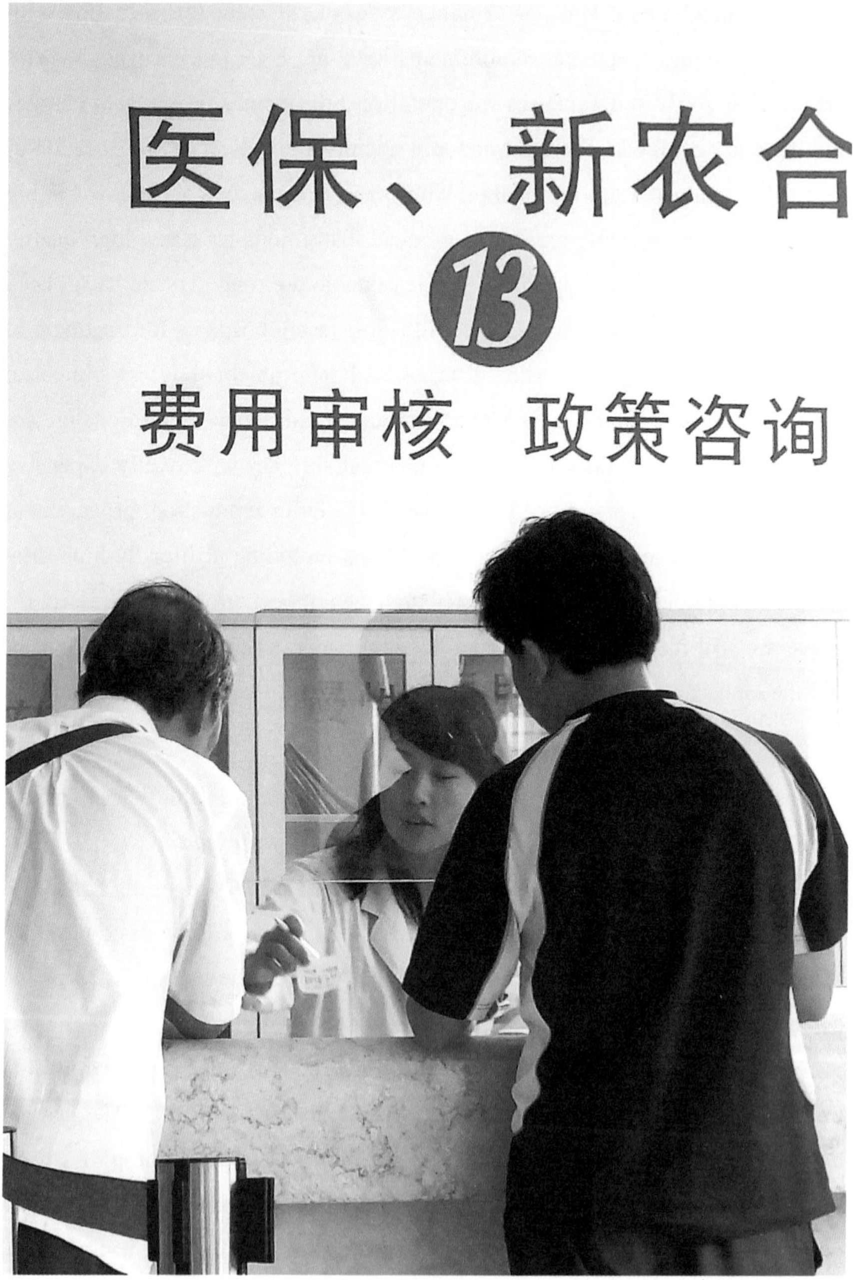

The medical and health care system has achieved some phased results in China, and its further reform is still in progress.

improvement of the essential drug system and reform in public hospitals. It requires effort to strengthen the fundamental role of basic medical insurance, intensify the public nature of medical services, optimize allocation of health resources, reconstruct the orders of drug production and circulation, improve the operational efficiency of the health system and accelerate formation of institutional security for people's access to medical services so as to improve the health conditions of all and make the fruits of the reform available to all. In terms of spending, the plan proposes that by 2015, growth in health spending will be reasonably controlled, with growth in government spending on health services higher than that in current fiscal spending, and the proportion of public health expenditure to current fiscal spending will gradually increase. As a result, the financial burden on people will be eased, the proportion of individual health expenditure to the total health expenses will fall to 30% or below, and medical services will be more accessible to the public.

The third plenary session of the 18th Central Committee of the CPC, held in 2013, further deployed methods to deepen the medical system reform in multiple aspects including medical security, medical services, public health, drug supply and the regulation system. According to the spirit of the *Decision of the CPC Central Committee on Several Major Issues Concerning Deepening the Reform in a Comprehensive Way*, one of the focuses for the next step is to advance the transformation of the medical insurance for all from framework shaping to institutional construction. To that end, efforts shall be made to expand the coverage of basic medical insurance, and to ensure the coverage rate reaches 95% or above, the per capita subsidy for urban residents under the medical insurance scheme and those under the new rural cooperative program will be RMB 360 or above and the proportion of reimbursement of hospitalization expenses covered by the policy scope will bearound 75%. Efforts shall be made to reform the methods of payment, advance real-time settlement and establish the mechanism for reimbursement of off-site medical treatment to make medical services more accessible to the public. Efforts shall be made to accelerate establishment of the serious disease insurance system for urban and rural residents and put in place a critical disease security mechanism for urban and rural residents. Efforts shall be made to improve the medical insurance management system, integrate the responsibilities of medical insurance management, drive reform in the operational mechanism and enhance operation efficiency and service quality. Commercial health insurance shall be vigorously developed to meet the diverse and multi-layered health demands of the public. Another focus of the reform is to consolidate at the grassroots level and advance the improvement of new mechanisms in grassoots medical institutions. Great efforts shall also be made to expand public hospital reform from pilot projects to nationwide implementation and do a good job in changing the situation in which hospitals subsidize their medical services with overly expensive drug prescriptions, innovating in institutions and arousing enthusiasm in medical staff. The key is to "clearly define governments' responsibilities" noted in the decision, to gradually eliminate profiting from drugs, to reform the mechanism for drug and consumable bidding and procurement, to deepen reform in the personnel system and distribution system, to establish a competitive employment mechanism and a performance assessment and distribution system that reflects public benefits and high efficiency and to make hospitals' internal management more scientific, regulated and intensive. The decision once again encourages hospital management via social forces and prioritizes support for setup of non-profit medical institutions. In China, whether or not social public welfare causes like schools or hospitals managed by social forces can be advanced lies primarily in the implementation of relevant policies.

China's Population Quality and Development of Human Resources

Education and health are major approaches to developing human resources through investment in human capital, and they directly determine the quality of a country's population. Superficially, education is reflected in residents' intelligence level, while health by their physical quality. Actually, education and health are mutually dependent and convertible. Well-educated people typically have higher demand for health services, and pay greater attention to disease prevention as well as diet, lifestyle and living environment. In 2012, former Director-General of the World Health Organization Dr. Zhong Daoheng said, "Most people do not die of disease, but of ignorance." Similarly, health is what all the success is based

Primary school students did long-distance running to greet the spring.

on. Just as Bill Gates said, "Health and high technologies pale in comparison with health." Generally, health paves the way for greater education.

Changes in the Literacy Rate and Per Capita Years of Schooling

Literacy rates and per capita years of schooling are important indicators to judge the education level of a country. Since 1949, China has attached great importance to eliminating illiteracy. On the eve of the victory over Japan in 1945, Mao Zedong, in his *On Coalition Government*, pointed out that "eliminating illiteracy in 80% of its population is a major task for New China." Work related to illiteracy elimination had started in liberated areas even before the war was over. At that time, 80% of the Chinese people were illiterate. Rural areas even had higher than 90% illiteracy and in some areas not a single literate person could be found at all. Improving the scientific and cultural quality of laborers was identified as fundamental to transforming China from a backward agricultural country to a modern industrial one.

After the founding of New China, the CPC and the Chinese government have introduced a wide range of measures. They organized anti-illiteracy campaigns among workers and peasants and worked to eliminate illiteracy nationwide in a planned and vigorous manner, with the aim to improve the cultural level of all laborers. On the eve of the 50th anniversary of New China, more than 200 million people had achieved literacy, with the adult illiteracy rate falling to a level lower than 15% and the illiteracy rate of young and middle-aged people below 5%. The United Nations Development Programme once concluded: "China has invested heavily in cultural development for a long time. As such, it falls into the category of medium cultural development level despite the low per capita income of residents. China's ranking by cultural development is quite different from its ranking by per capita GNP, or 49 points, which indicates China has wisely used its national income."21 But with a weak base, a big population

Great efforts were made to enhance the educational training for farmers in China.

and vast land, China has experienced unbalanced development between urban and rural areas and among different regions. In the third national census launched in 1982, there were still 236 million illiterate and semi-illiterate (those who know a few words at the age of 12 or above) people in China's 29 provinces, municipalities and autonomous regions. The average total schooling among those aged 25 and above was 4.3 years, 0.6 year shorter than the world's average level (4.9 years) at that time.

China restored its college entrance examination system in the early years of its reform and opening-up. Moreover, it promulgated the Compulsory Education Law and the Regulations on the Elimination of Illiteracy, and set the strategic goal of "basically eliminating illiteracy among young and middle-aged people and basically popularizing nine-year compulsory education (basically popularizing primary school education in the 1980s and popularizing junior middle school education in areas where possible)". As a result, great headway was made in

Table 5-3-1
Change in the Illiteracy Rate of Population Aged 15 and Above in China and Other Parts of the World
(Unit: %)

	1960	**1970**	**1980**	**1990**	**1995**	**2000**	**Changes**
							1980–2000
Worldwide (109)	36.4	31.4	29.5	26.4	26.1	24.2	-5.3
Developing countries (73)	64.1	56.1	49.7	41.7	38.3	34.4	-15.3
Developed countries (23)	6.1	5.1	4.8	4.5	3.8	3.7	-1.1
Transitional countries (13)	4.5	3.1	2.8	1.7	2.1	2.2	-0.6
East Asia and Pacific (10)	52.5	35.4	22.6	26.4	22.5	19.8	-2.8
China	–	–	22.8a	15.9	12.0	6.7	-16.1
South Asia (7)	74.3	69.3	66.9	55.2	51.2	45.2	-21.7
Middle East and North Africa (11)	81.0	69.8	55.5	42.8	36.0	32.0	-23.5
Saharan Africa (22)	68.9	63.8	56.8	45.9	44.5	42.8	-14.0
Latin America (23)	37.9	31.2	23.8	17.2	15.8	14.6	-9.2

Note: a is the data in 1982.
Data source: 1. Barro, R. J. and J. W. Lee (2000), *International Data on Educational Attainment: Updates and Implications*, CID Working Paper No.42, April, p.29.
2. Website of the National Bureau of Statistics of the People's Republic of China.

Table 5-3-2
Changes in the Average Years of Schooling for the Population Aged 15 and Above in China and Other Parts of the World
(Unit: %)

	1960	1970	1980	1990	1995	2000	Growth
							1980–2000
Worldwide (109)	4.64	5.16	5.92	6.43	6.44	6.66	1.13
Developing countries (73)	2.05	2.67	3.57	4.42	4.79	5.13	1.44
Developed countries (23)	7.06	7.56	8.86	9.19	9.52	9.76	1.10
Transitional countries (13)	7.42	8.47	8.90	9.97	9.45	9.68	1.09
East Asia and Pacific (10)	2.83	3.80	5.10	5.84	6.35	6.71	1.32
China a			5.33b	6.40	-	7.79	1.46
South Asia (7)	1.51	2.05	2.97	3.85	4.16	4.57	1.54
Middle East and North Africa (11)	1.23	2.07	3.29	4.38	4.98	5.44	1.65
Saharan Africa (22)	1.74	2.07	2.39	3.14	3.39	3.52	1.47
Latin America (23)	3.30	3.83	4.43	5.32	5.74	6.06	1.37

Note: a is sourced from the Analysis Report on the Cultural Quality of China's Population released by the National Center for Educational Development Research, December 2003; b is the data in 1982.

Data source: Barro, R. J. and J. W. Lee (2000), *International Data on Educational Attainment: Updates and Implications*, CID Working Paper No.42, April, p.29.

Table 5-3-3
Proportion of the Population Receiving Higher Education in China and Other Parts of the World
(Unit: %)

	1960	1970	1980	1990	1995	2000	Growth
							1980–2000
Worldwide (109)	3.3	5.0	7.5	10.3	11.3	12.6	1.7
Developing countries (73)	0.8	1.7	3.1	4.6	5.7	6.5	2.1
Developed countries (23)	6.7	9.9	15.8	22.4	24.8	27.1	1.7
Transitional countries (13)	3.8	6.3	7.7	11.2	11.4	13.9	1.8
East Asia and Pacific (10)	1.6	2.7	5.0	7.4	10.0	11.7	2.3
China	—	—	0.6a	1.4	2.0	3.6	6.0
South Asia (7)	0.4	1.2	2.1	2.9	3.3	3.7	1.8
Middle East and North Africa (11)	0.9	1.7	3.6	5.6	7.2	8.8	2.4
Saharan Africa (22)	0.2	0.8	0.6	1.3	2.1	2.2	3.7
Latin America (23)	1.8	2.5	5.2	8.2	9.5	10.9	2.1

Note: a is data in 1982.
Data source:
1. Barro, R. J. and J. W. Lee (2000), *International Data on Educational Attainment: Updates and Implications*, CID Working Paper No.42, April, p.29.
2. Website of the National Bureau of Statistics of the People's Republic of China.

education. Table 5-3-1, Table 5-3-2 and Table 5-3-3 show that during 1980-2000, the decline in the illiteracy rate of China's population aged 15 and above was three times the global average, slightly higher than the level in other developing countries yet lower than the level in South Asia, Middle East and North African countries. The increase in the average years of schooling of China's population aged 15 and above was higher than the global average and basically the same as in other developing countries. The proportion of China's population receiving higher education grew rapidly, with growth reaching multiples of that of other countries and the global average. Horizontal comparison suggests that in 2000, the illiteracy rate of China's population aged 15 and above was far higher than that in transitional countries and developed countries, but was only 27.7% of the global average and 19.5% of the average in developing countries; The average years of schooling of China's population aged 15 and above fell slightly short of the level in transitional countries and developed countries, but was well above the global average. However, the proportion of China's population receiving

The celebration for graduation by the undergraduates in Tsinghua University.

higher education remained low, only representing 55.4% of the average level for developing countries and 28.6% of the global average, and similar to the levels found in South Asian countries.

Since the 21st century, and the 16th CPC National Congress in particular, China has increased spending on education to ease the financial burdens on citizens and made tremendous efforts to promote education equality. The sixth national population census in 2010 showed that the education level of China's population improved significantly. The number of young and middle-aged illiterate Chinese aged 15-50 decreased from 20.55 million in 2000 to 8.52 million, a reduction of 12.03 million. The illiteracy rate of young and middle-aged people fell by 1.72 percentage points to 1.08% from 2.80% in 2000. The illiteracy rate of population aged 15 and above was 4.1%, a decrease of more than 30%. The average period of schooling of China's population aged 15 and above increased by 1.26 years to 9.05 years, compared with 7.79 years in 2000, indicating the average education level had reached senior middle school education. In 1990, the average period of schooling of China's population aged 25 and above was 5.8 years, basically the same as the global average.The figure was 7.4 years in 2000, 0.6 year higher than the global average (6.8 years), and 8.6 years in 2010, well above the global average (7.4 years). The average period of schooling of the newly-added labor force improved by two years to 12.7 years in 2010, compared with 10.9 years in 2005. As for educational structure, China has experienced a trend in which those only achieving primary school education dwindled, those receiving secondary education maintain a stable level and those receiving higher education grew quickly. In 2010, the average period of schooling of individuals aged 25 and above was 12.4 years (equivalent to the first-year college level) in the US, and 11.6 years (equivalent to the third-year senior middle school level) in Japan, which were 3.4 years and 2.6 years longer than the level in China, respectively, indicating the proportion of China's population receiving junior college education and above remained low. In 2009, the proportion of individuals aged 25-64 receiving higher education in OECD

countries comprised 30.0% of the total population, over ı.
(9.7%) in China in 2010. By age, Chinese aged 55–64 who had ı
education (in the late 1970s and early 1980s) accounted for 3.6%, w.
aged 25–34 receiving higher education represented 17.9%, about five ı.
greater than those aged 55–64.The 10-year gap between the two groups indicates the notably faster pace in the development of China's higher education in the 21st century.

Changes in Life Expectancy and Relevant Indicators

Average life expectancy is an effective benchmarkfor judging the health level of a population. Other metrics include the infant mortality rate and maternal mortality rate.

The World Bank estimates that from 1960 to 1980, the average life expectancy of Chinese residents increased by 27 years, compared with 15 years in low-income countries, nine years in middle-income countries and four years in industrialized countries during the same period. As 1960 was the hardest year in New China's history, the per capita life expectancy for that year was not representative. However, it is an indisputable fact that the growth in life expectancy in China has been among the world's highest levels for a long period of since the founding of New China. The World Bank economic mission published a report after visiting China in which it stated that during the period of 1950-1980, China outperformed other developing countries in terms of growth ofper capita life expectancy (an increase of 28 years in life expectancy, compared with 15 years in low-income countries). Moreover, the life expectancy of Chinese people also exceeded the average level of middle-income countries, and was 16 years longer than the levels found in countries of similar income levels. At the same time, China saw significant drops in the infant mortality rate and maternal mortality rate. Table 5-3-4 shows that the mortality rate of children under five was 37.6% in 1980, which was 47% of the world's average level and 27.2% of the level in China in 1950. Experts attributed the achievement mainly to China's unique medical security system. The report by the World Bank economic mission noted that "China's introduction of the cooperative medical system in rural areas is the only practice in developing countries to provide health security." The report also said that "primary health care was mainly inspired by China, which developed a successful grassroots health care system in rural areas that account for 80% of its total population to provide people with affordable and appropriate health care services and meet the basic health demands of most people. The model is very suitable for developing countries." China's practices received unanimous recognition from international organizations, and WHO and UNICEF recommended the "Chinese model" to other developing countries on multiple occasions. Of course, China's success in health care was not the only reason for the rapid improvement in people's health conditions, which was also ascribed to improvements in education, sufficient supply and even distribution of food as well as improvements in water supply and health facilities. That said, this medical security system that centers on prevention and features low costs and wide coverage has certainly made an immeasurable contribution.

But this momentum didn't continue after China's reform began. During the 1980s and 1990s, reductions in the infant mortality rate and especially the life expectancy of China's population slowed down as a result of the collapse of the original medical security system and particularly the lack of medical security for rural residents. From 1957 to 1981, China's average life expectancy increased annually by 0.45 year from 57 years to 67.9 years. From 1981 to 1990, life expectancy increased by 0.7 year in total, or shorter than 0.08 year annually, to 68.6 years. From 1990 to 2000, the average life expectancy increased by 0.28 year in total, or fewer than 0.03 year annually, to 71.4 years. Due to unfair and uneven distribution of public health resources, nearly 100 million people had no access to medical services in 2000, over 30 million poor people could not access timely medical assistance, and nearly 20% of China's rural counties failed to meet the goal of "everyone having access to primary healthcare services in

2000". Clean water was unavailable to more than 100 million people and tap water unavailable to over 400 million rural people The rate of sewage treatment was only 28.5% in rural areas. The goal of lowering the maternal mortality rate and incidence rate was not achieved. Nine provinces in southwest and northwest China reported an average maternal mortality rate of up to 177.96/100,000, 2.8 times the average level in China (56.2/100,000), well above the goal of 47.4/100,000 and similar to the level in African countries. In China had 8% of infants were not provided with vaccinations, 13% in poor rural areas, and the goal of bringing the neonatal tetanus rate to 1% or lower was not achieved. Work related to disease prevention and health care was poorly implemented, with many provinces in central and western China still reporting high disease incidence rates and relatively short life expectancies. Health expenditures at various levels and total health expenses were both lower than planned goals and the minimum standards required by the WHO and there were problems implementing subsidies

The acceleration of aging in China: 15% citizens have been the people aged over 60.

Table 5-3-4
International Comparison of Infant Mortality Rates and Average Life Expectancy

Year	Mortality Rate for Infants Aged 0–4 years (‰)						Average Life Expectancy (years)					
	Worldwide	China	US	India	Nigeria	Singapore	Worldwide	China	US	India	Japan	Nigeria
1950	—	138.4	—	—	—	—	—	48.0	—	—	—	—
1970	—	51.5	20.1	137.0	139.0	20.5	—	64.1	—	—	—	—
1980	80.0	37.6	12.6	129.1	124.1	11.7	62.7	67.9	73.7	54.3	76.0	45.9
1990	63.9	32.9	9.4	80.0	120.0	6.7	65.2	68.6	75.2	59.1	78.8	46.4
2000	57.6	28.4	6.9	68.0	107.0	2.9	66.6	71.4	77.0	62.9	81.1	43.8
2006	49.5	20.1	6.5	57.4	98.6	2.3	68.2	72.0	77.8	64.5	82.3	46.8

Note: Data in 1950 and 1970 were those during 1950-1954 and 1970-1974, respectively; Data in 1980 were those in 1981.

Data source: *Mortality data of China's population*, compiled by Huang Rongqing and Liu Yan and published by China Population Publishing House in 1995; International Statistical Yearbook (Electronic edition) 1996, 1998 and 2008; Data from the fifth national census and China 1% Population Survey Data 2005 (Electronic edition).

Figure 5-3-1
Changes in China's Per Capita Life Expectancy

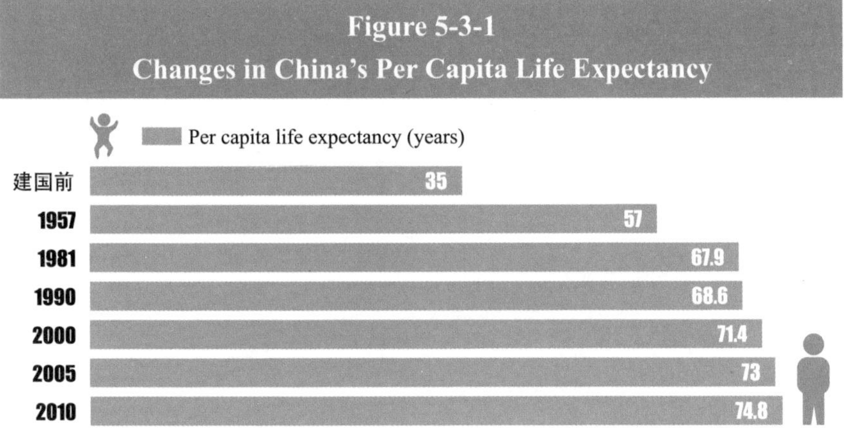

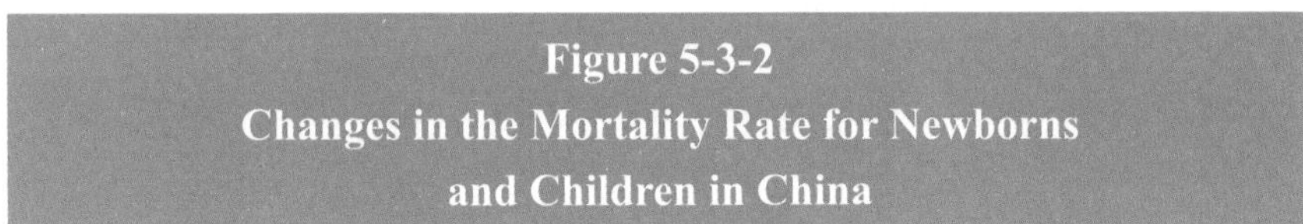

Figure 5-3-2
Changes in the Mortality Rate for Newborns and Children in China

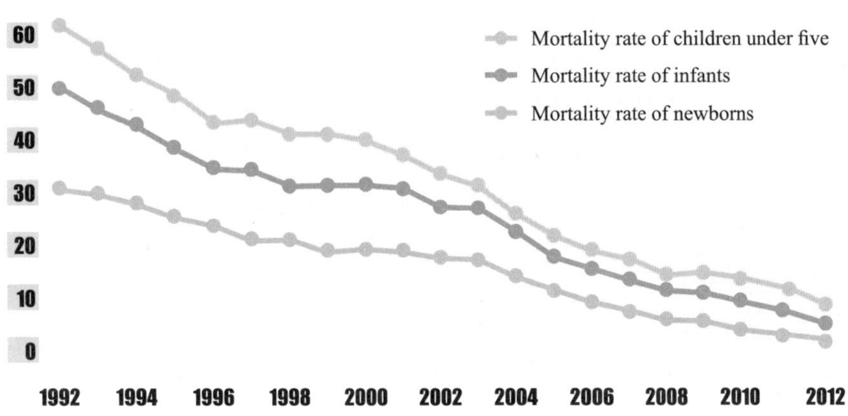

for health care services. As it happened, China chose incorrect practices when exploring market-oriented reforms in both the medical and education fields, with the former's path more winding than the latter's.

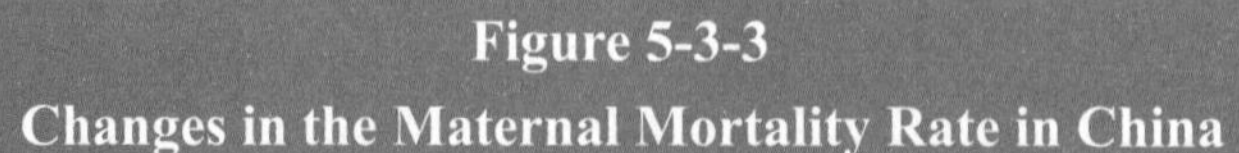

Figure 5-3-3

Changes in the Maternal Mortality Rate in China

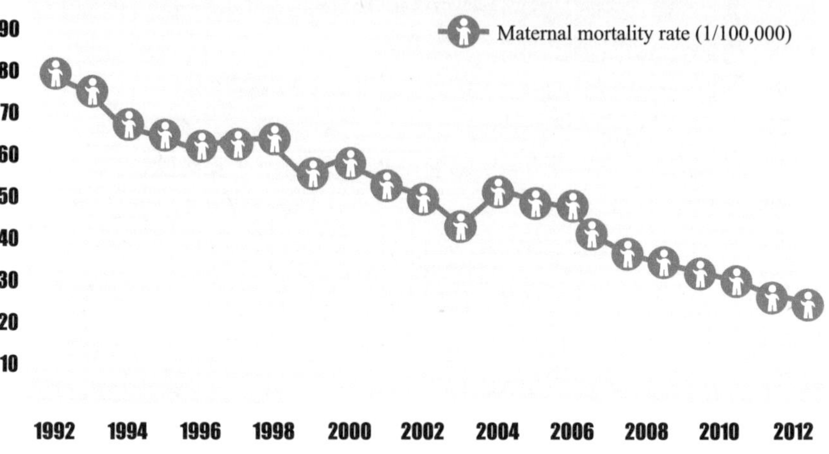

Since the 21st century, and especially the 16th CPC National Congress, China has worked to improve the people's livelihoods, significantly increasing health care spending and gradually taking the medical system reform onto the right path. Consequently, residents' health conditions improved. From 2002 to 2011, the maternal mortality rate fell from 51.3/100,000 to 26.1/100,000, the infant mortality rate from 29.2‰ to 12.1‰, and the mortality rate of children under five from 34.9‰ to 15.6‰. In 2010, average life expectancy reached 74.8 years, up 3.4 years from 71.4 years in 2000, and growth was noticeably faster than the previous two decades. China has taken the lead among developing countries but still lags behind developed countries in terms of its citizens' health conditions. Data from UNICEF showed that in 2007, China ranked the 107th among 193 countries sorted in descending orderin terms of mortality rate of children under five, near the middle of the pack globally and behind both Thailand (156th) and Vietnam (126th). In 2008 China's maternal mortality rate was notably lower than that in Brazil, India and South Africa and basically the same as that in Russia, but only equivalent to the level of the US in 1965 (31.6/100,000). According to WHO data, China's ranking in terms of maternal mortality rate jumped from the 97th in 1990 to the 109th in 2005 (in a descending order), near the middle in global terms. In 2010, the world's average life expectancy was 69.6 years, with high-income countries at 79.8 years and middle-income countries at 69.1 years. Life expectancy in China was nearly six years longer than that of middle-income countries, but five years shorter than that of high-income countries.

Nutrition and Health

People's physical health is subject to a variety of factors, with inheritance and daily nutrition possibly the most important ones besides basic medical security. In recent years, the WHO has assessed the numerous factors that affect human health. The results show that inheritance tops the list with a 15% contribution and is followed by dietary nutrition (13%) and medical services (8%). Inheritance is a biological factor and is difficult to change in the short term. Environmental factors are equally hard to reverse, as takes a long time for to address pollution and ecological degradation. However, lifestyles can be improved via changes or participation in dietary nutrition, food safety, sports, health awareness and psychology. The famous Victoria Declaration put forth the four cornerstone approach to a healthy way of life, i.e. a reasonable diet, regular exercise, no tobacco and less alcohol and a balanced psychology, with a reasonable diet topping the list in importance.

For a reasonable diet, we must reasonably match different kinds of food in quality, quantity and proportion based on the roles of various types of nutrition and in line with hygienic requirements, with the aim to strike a balance between the nutritional needs and nutritional intake of human bodies. An unreasonable diet will lead to inadequate or excessive nutrition and trigger a chain of diseases. Before China's reforms, people's diet structure was high in carbohydrates and low in protein. It was also low in fat and vitamins due to the shortage of food, non-staple foodstuff in particular, and diseases caused by

inadequate nutrition were widespread. However, the life of the Chinese people has changed tremendously after the reforms. Both urban and rural residents enjoy a growing variety of food, with grain consumption declining and meat consumption increasing. The diet structure in Western or wealthy countries has become increasingly favored, with food rich in energy, fat and protein replacing food rich in dietary fiber. Consequently, residents in many areas, especially cities, are increasingly plagued by diseases caused by overnutrition such as obesity, diabetes, hypertension, angiocardiopathy and cancer, while residents in poor areas may still suffer from inadequate nutrition.

Changes in the dietary structure are an inevitable outcome of social and economic progress. But the problem is that human bodies cannot adapt to the excessively rapid changing of people's dietary structure, resulting in a higher morbidity rate and mortality rate of non-infectious chronic diseases compared with those in developed countries. China presently has 260 million people suffering from chronic diseases. Deaths caused by chronic diseases account for

The community public outreach activities about medical kits for families was held in Beijing.

85% of the death total and the burden of such diseases represents 70% of the total burden of disease. The dietary structure has far-reaching influence on average life expectancy.

Increased marketization also has also triggered many changes in lifestyles, such as an accelerated pace of life, mounting work pressures and increasing height and weight among youngsters, who also tend to exercise less than before. Despite outstanding achievements in competitive sports, China sees a low level of sports among its citizenry and the gap is even larger between urban and rural areas. Therefore, the Chinese government released the *National Fitness Regulations and National Fitness Program* in a bid to promote the coordinated development of national fitness and competitive sports and advocate healthy and civilized ways of life. China also raised the bar for physical exercise among students on campuses.

Meanwhile, chronic disease control has been intensified. Since 2002, the focus of disease control has gradually shifted from treatment to a combination

Prevention of diabetes on campus in Yongchuan District, Chongqing City.

of both prevention and treatment, with control networks jointly established by disease control institutions, grassroots medical institutions, hospitals and professional control institutions coming into existence. Construction of state-level demonstration areas for chronic disease control has been initiated and campaigns including the National Health Promotion Project for Hundreds of Million Chinese Farmers, Community Health Promotion, Health Literacy Promotion and China Health Knowledge Promotion Incentive Plan, have been carried out. A health education system covering both urban and rural residents has been put in place with joint efforts from multiple sectors and participation across society.

Nutrition guidance is also a major field that the government can work on. Japan boasts the world's longest life expectancy, as its cuisine combines the merits of Eastern and Western diets by reasonably matching vegetables with animal proteins. Additionally, the government offers effective guidance on

A nutrition publicity week in Beijing, advocating balanced diet.

dietary proportion, food composition and consumption structures. Following the release of the *Outline of China's Food Structure Reform and Development in the 1990s* in February 1993 and the *Outline of the Program for Food and Nutrition Development (2001–2010)* in November 2001, China further promulgated the *Outline of the Program for Food and Nutrition Development (2014–2020)* in February 2014, demonstrating the new levels of food consumption, nutrition improvement and dietary composition of the Chinese people who have entered a well-off society while marking the ongoing great changes in ideas about food consumption, knowledge about nutrition and health and lifestyles of Chinese citizens. The program the Chinese government has implemented since the autumn of 2011 in poor areas to improve the nutritional status of rural students under compulsory education has also been impressive. According to reports of the Ministry of Education, by the end of October 2013, nearly 100,000 schools in 699 state-level pilot counties (including 19 farms in the Xinjiang Production and Construction Corps) in 22 pilot programs nationwide offered meals, benefiting 22.4 million students. In addition, 529 counties in 19 provinces carried out local pilot projects, covering 40,000 schools and benefiting 10 million students. More than one third of Chinese counties introduced programs to improve students' nutritional status, and over one fourth of rural students under compulsory education enjoy nutrition subsidies. Health education and nutrition intervention, including the family planning policy (especially maternal care as well as prenatal and postnatal care) which has been implemented for a long time, have increased people's health awareness and improved their ways of life, while playing an important role in improving the quality of human resources in China.

Goals of Human Resources Development to Promote Future Education and Health

China is the world's largest developing country, with development in education and health greatly improving the cultural and physical quality of 1.3

billion Chinese people and contributing significantly to economic development, social progress and improvement in people's livelihood. But China still has a long way to go before achieving the transformation from a country with a big population to one with a competitive talent pool. Chinese people's cultural quality is far from meeting the needs for scientific and technological innovation and their health conditions remain unbalanced. Development of China's education and health is still insufficient to fulfill the goals of building China into a well-off society and catching up the levels in developed economies.

Accordingly, the Chinese government has set the goals for human resources development during the 12th Five-year Plan period and by 2020. As for education, during the 12th Five-year Plan period, efforts will be made to comprehensively improve the capability of education in serving modernization and the all-round development of people so as to basically achieve education modernization and build China into a learning-oriented society by 2020, as well as laying a sound

More and more people have consciously developed a healthy and civilized lifestyle in China.

foundation for China to become a human resource superpower. As for health, a basic health system that covers both urban and rural residents will be established, making medical services more accessible, efficient and satisfactory. Efforts shall also be made to lower the financial burdens of individuals in need of medical treatment, narrow the gap in allocation of health resources among regions and health conditions among different groups, provide every resident with access to medical services in case of illness and improve the average life expectancy by one year from 2010. Detailed indicators are shown in Table 5-3-5.

Table 5-3-5
Main Objectives for Development of Human Resources

Indicators	Unit	2009	2015	2020
Number of those receiving higher education	10,000 people	9830	14500	19500
Average years of schooling of main working-age population	Year	9.5	10.5	11.2
Including: Proportion of those receiving higher education	%	9.9	15.0	20.0
Average years of schooling of newly-increased laborers	Year	12.4	13.3	13.5
Including: Proportion of those receiving senior middle school education or higher	%	67.0	87.0	90.0
Average life expectancy	%	73.5—74.8 (1)	74.5—75.8 (2)	77—80 (3)
Infant mortality rate	‰	13.8	≤12	≤10
Mortality rate of children under five	‰	17.2	≤14	≤13
Maternal mortality rate	10 Million	31.9	≤22	≤20

Note:

1. is the data in 2010. Official data include 73.5 years and 74.8 years, with the latter from the sixth national census;
2. The goal set in the 12th Five-year Plan is an increase of one year from 2010;
3. 77 years is from *Healthy China 2020: Strategic Research Report* (August 2012); 80 years was calculated by scholars, such as *China 2030: Heading for Common Prosperity* by Hu Angang, published by China Renmin University Press in 2011. Other data are from the *Outline of China's Long and Medium-term Plan on Education Reform and Development (2010-2020)*, July 29, 2010, and the *Plan of the Ministry of Health on Implementing the Outline of China for Development of Women and Children*, February 17, 2012.

Notes

20. At the event to celebrate the 100th anniversary of Peking University on May 4, 1998, Jiang Zemin announced that "China shall have a number of world-class universities to realize modernization." To implement the strategy of the CPC Central Committee on invigorating China through science and education and Jiang Zemin's call, the Ministry of Education decided to prioritize support for selected schools of higher learning, including Peking University and Tsinghua University in their efforts to develop into world-class and high-level universities during implementation of the National Program of Action for Educational Revitalization toward the 21st Century, which was called Project 985.

21. UNDP, Human Development Report 1994, New York: Oxford University Press, 1994, pp.105–100.

Conclusion

It is not realistic to clearly introduce every detail of Chinese society in this book without risking becoming excessively verbose. The writer has simply focused on key aspects. Some areas not elaborated in this book, such as the people's life, may have been reflected in the chapter about economy. Readers can learn about and judge the huge changes and progresses in China's society in combination with the content of this entire series of books.

China's society has experienced tremendous changes in the past and present, and will embrace new ones in the future. The international community generally refers to the former Soviet Union and East European countries after the Cold War as transitional countries, as they not only have undergone changes in social natures, but also are moving from planned economies to market economies. Actually, compared with such countries, China is a more typical transitional country, as a more influential transition is taking place in this developing country with vast land area and a large population that comprises one fifth of the world's total. China is moving from a planned economy to a market economy, morphing from an agricultural power into an industrial power, changing from the "world's factory" to a higher-value producer, moving from extensive sprawl to intensive development that features resources conservation and environmental protection, all while heading toward increased urbanization, modernization, globalization and informatization. All of this is bringing drastic and rapid changes to this huge economy. The new achievements China makes every day are giving rise to new problems all the time.

In this book, the writer uses lots of data in the form of tables or figures to let the readers see the changes in as an intuitive and precise manner as possible, whie introducing vertical comparison to show progress and horizontal comparison to indicate the gaps. Moreover, these comparisons make it clearer that most problems currently facing China are those resulting from rapid social transformation, including either insufficient development or unbalanced development.

The UNDP established the Human Development Index (HDI) in 1990, with the aim to underline that human development is the ultimate goal of development. After adjustment, the HDI currently includes four indicators, i.e. life expectancy at birth, average years of schooling, expected years of schooling and per capita national income. The Human Development Report 2013 published by the UNDP shows that China's HDI was 0.699 in 2012, significantly up from 0.407 in 1980 and an average annual growth of 1.7%. The index was always higher than the average level in countries in the East Asia and Pacific region (0.683) and the average level of BRIC countries (0.655), and put China at the 101st position among 187 countries/regions surveyed by the UN. Concretely speaking, among all the HDI indicators, the life expectancy at birth of China's population went up by 6.7 years from 1980, the average years of schooling up 3.8 years, expected years of schooling up 3.3 years and the per capita national income up 1,416%. However, China's HDI ranking was 11 spots behind its ranking by per capita national income, indicating the huge imbalance in China's development process.

After adjusted for internal inequality in health, education and income, China's HDI was 0.543, with a loss ratio of 22.4% (but its ranking remained 101st). In particular, the loss ratios of the education and income indices were respectively 23.2% and 29.5%, underscoring the serious inequality in China's development.

Imbalance and inequality between urban and rural areas and among different regions, fields and classes are the challenges that China must address in its future development and are key to China's attempt to cross the "middle income trap" and successful completion of its all-round transformation. Promoting social fairness and justice and ensuring that all people share the fruits of development in a fairer way are the focuses of the decision on deepening China's reform made by the third plenary session of the 18th Central Committee of the CPC. Undoubtedly, as a developing country with more than 1.3 billion people, China must make consistent and arduous efforts to fulfill the goal it has set. Also obvious is that China's reform and development will benefit not only the Chinese people but people of all the other countries.